FOREWORD

One of the more noteworthy trends in financial markets over the past two decades has been securitisation, the issuance of mortgage-backed and asset-backed securities, *i.e.* securities supported not by the credit standing of a private corporation or public sector entity but by specific assets.

Securitisation is one manifestation of a development in the financial systems of OECD countries in which on-balance sheet bank lending is being replaced by direct intermediation through capital markets. Although commercial banks and investment banks actively develop and distribute these securities, the assets supporting the securities do not appear on their balance sheets.

Markets in these securities are particularly well developed in the United States where their volume already approaches $2 trillion, comparable to that of US Treasury securities. In several other countries, significant activity is already taking place while governments and/or private institutions are seeking to promote the use of securitisation.

In order to understand the causes of the expansion of securitisation, to analyse its impact on the structure and soundness of financial systems and to assess the prospects for wider issuance of mortgage-backed and asset-backed securities in OECD countries, the OECD's Committee on Financial Markets commissioned this enquiry. This study examines the underlying forces in financial systems that have encouraged the growth of securitisation in some Member countries and also analyses why securitisation has advanced so far in a few markets, notably the United States, while making only limited progress elsewhere. The study compares "off-balance-sheet securitisation" (issuance of mortgage-backed and asset-backed securities) with more traditional "on-balance-sheet securitisation" (*i.e.* mortgage bonds). The phenomenon of securitisation is examined both in terms of dynamic trends in the financial markets of OECD countries as well as in terms of legal, regulatory and institutional factors that have influenced the progress of securitisation.

This study benefitted from comments from members of the OECD's Committee on Financial Markets and is published on the responsibility of the Secretary-General of the OECD.

3

TABLE OF CONTENTS

Chapter 1

INTRODUCTION AND SUMMARY

One of the more prominent developments in international finance in the past two decades, and one which could assume even greater importance in the future is securitisation, by which is meant the issuance of marketable securities backed not by the expected capacity to repay of a private corporation or public sector entity, but by the expected cash flows from specific assets. This study examines the forces that have led market participants to undertake securitisation, traces its development in OECD Member countries, and assesses the prospects for further development.

At the outset, it should be stated that the term "securitisation" has been used in two basic ways in the past few years. Through the mid-1980s, it referred to the broad trend in financial intermediation of replacing traditional lending by banks with the issuing of securities. More recently, the term has been used more narrowly to refer to the issue of mortgage-backed and asset-backed securities process that can be characterised as "off-balance-sheet securitisation"; that since the assets supporting the securities are removed from the balance sheet of the originating institution, or in some cases never appear on the balance sheet of the originator. In keeping with market practice, this second sense will be used here unless otherwise specified.

In off-balance-sheet securitisation, a financial institution (commercial or investment bank) is usually active in structuring and marketing the security, but the institution's responsibilities for the payments on it are strictly limited. These securities are placed with investors, whose decision whether to purchase them is to a large degree separate from the credit standing of the originating institution; the decision instead depends on both the investor's assessment of the capacity of the underlying assets to generate the cash flows needed to meet contractual principal and interest payments, and the degree of protection incorporated in the structure of the security itself.

It is worth remembering that in addition to the "off-balance-sheet" variety a number of Member countries have well-established systems of "on-balance-sheet securitisation". In particular, several European countries have well-developed markets in asset-related bonds many of which have been in existence for decades. The most common of these are mortgage bonds, mainly by residential mortgages. A similar security is the "communal bond" supported by receivables from local authorities. Mortgage and/or communal bonds are extremely important in some domestic markets, notably Germany, Denmark, Norway and Sweden. The function of these asset-related instruments, which are usually issued by specialised financial institutions, is to allow the issuing institution to engage in on-balance-sheet lending for comparatively long periods at fixed rates while avoiding the kind of interest rate mismatches that would occur if a portfolio of long-term assets were funded with shorter-term deposits. In issuing these bonds, the institution transfers the market risks inherent in long-term assets to investors. At the same time, investors have an attractive long-term fixed-rate asset. Thus, these securities fulfil some of the same functions as mortgage-backed or asset-backed securities. However, since the asset remains on the balance sheet, the originating institution retains the credit risk.

The outstanding volume of mortgage and communal bonds in Europe approaches $1 trillion equivalent, a sum far in excess of mortgage-backed and asset-backed securities in all countries other than the United States. Furthermore, some international investors have shown interest in these assets. On the whole, however, only a limited amount of cross-border business in these instruments has taken place, and few OECD countries have shown interest in introducing new domestic systems based upon on-balance-sheet securitisation. While this study will focus mainly on off-balance sheet securitisation in order to reflect the current concerns of analysts and market participants, alternate means of using asset-related securities as a financing technique will also be considered.

The most widely used assets in off-balance-sheet securitisation are residential mortgages, credit card receivables, automobile loans and other consumer receivables. These assets are normally found in large homogeneous pools for which historical data can be used to estimate probable default rates. In the United States and in the international markets, the term "asset-backed security" (ABS) is used to mean securities backed by any asset except mortgages. Securities backed or "collateralised" by residential mortgages are called "mortgage-backed securities" (MBS). Both of these terms typically refer to off-balance-sheet operations.

In securitisation, an "originator" creates a legal entity known as a "Special Purpose Vehicle" (SPV) and sells "receivables" to the SPV. The purpose of the SPV is to isolate the receivables and the associated cash flows from the originator and to perform certain other closely related operations (restructuring of cash flows, credit enhancement, etc.). Legal agreements delineate the rights and obligations of the investors, the originators and other participants in the operation. The probability of credit problems, as well as the legal structure of the proposed operation, is assessed by credit rating agencies which assign a rating. The SPV issues the securities, which are sold to investors.

Initially, these securities were created to promote residential mortgage finance in the United States in the 1970s. In the 1980s, the techniques developed in the mortgage market were applied to an increasingly wide variety of assets. Such securities are now major instruments in the capital market of the United States. Many observers had expected this technique to spread to many other countries, and indeed this happened in a few countries, particularly where the legal and regulatory systems are similar to those of the United States, (the United Kingdom, Canada and Australia) and in the euro-markets. In a few other countries (*e.g.* France), private financial institutions perceived the advantages of such techniques, but also saw the problems of introducing them under existing domestic laws and regulations; partly as a result, the authorities began to introduce changes in domestic laws to make wider securitisation possible.

Despite sustained efforts by officials and private market participants in many countries to promote its development, one of the striking features of securitisation in an international perspective is the imbalance between the huge proportion of the MBS and ABS markets in the United States and their rather modest proportions everywhere else. Indeed, one of the central questions concerning securitisation in a global context is whether this technique will remain of marginal significance outside the United States, or whether other OECD countries are likely to experience growth in this area in the future.

Clearly, the exceptionally strong expansion of securitisation in the United States reflects factors peculiar to that country: *inter alia,* special federal programmes to develop mortgage financing, the tradition of fixed-rate mortgages, and large numbers of geographically dispersed banks. Other explanatory factors include the rising share of capital markets in intermediation, the presence of a sophisticated community of institutional investors, the diminishing availability of low-cost deposits for funding, the decline of the savings and loan sector, and strains on the balance sheets of banks in the 1980s. Indeed, one of the main reasons for the rapid advance of securitisation in the United States is that in the late 1980s, banks in that country adopted strategies based upon shifting emphasis away from traditional lending, consequently, the size of bank balance sheets in the United States, and particularly the volumes of loans by American banks, grew appreciably less rapidly than in other OECD countries.

A number of forces conducive to securitisation in the United States seem to be present in other OECD countries as well. Hypothetically, one can immediately identify some possible advantages of securitisation. Securitisation makes it possible to obtain long-term fixed rate financing for certain activities, particularly housing, while minimising interest rate risk to the originator. This is accomplished by passing the interest rate risk and other market risks in mortgage finance to investors seeking long-term fixed rate assets. Capital market participants can create new categories of securities that match investor risk/return objectives. Securitisation is thus also a reflection of the growing importance of institutional investors as holders of wealth who seek a wide range of assets in order to achieve their desired risk/return objectives.

Securitisation can be seen as one aspect of a wider transformation in OECD countries in which an increasing share of financial intermediation is taking place through capital markets as opposed to bank lending. Although the process of securitisation in the form of asset sales to SPVs represents a displacement of the banking system by direct recourse of borrowers to investors in the capital market, the commercial banks in the United States and in some other countries have been instrumental in promoting these products. This phenomenon in turn reflects a number of trends in the banking industry, including a shift to transactions-oriented banking and a desire to de-emphasize traditional lending as a source of bank earnings. Furthermore, with increasing recognition by market participants and regulators of the importance of maintaining adequate levels of capitalisation and making efficient use of bank capital, securitisation can represent an important addition to the tools available to financial institutions for asset and liability management. By reducing the size of assets and earning more income from fees, banks can earn higher income from any given level of capital. In combination with other risk management techniques, particularly derivatives, securitisation can greatly enhance the capability of management control the size and structure of balance sheets and, more generally, to structure and control risk.

In addition to generally assisting the management of banks, securitisation may be an effective means of addressing specific problems within the financial sector, particularly for depository institutions which have experienced declines in balance sheet quality and/ or which hold large amounts of impaired assets. In some cases, asset sales may be the most efficient way of improving capital/asset ratios, and securitisation may be the most effective way to effect such sales. Moreover, securitisation may be a more cost-effective means of funding than borrowing in the money market, particularly for banks that have been downgraded by credit rating agencies but have high-quality receivables.

Securitisation can be a useful mechanism for dealing with impaired assets and can be useful in rehabilitating financial institutions which have become insolvent. In some cases banks have found that selectively removing impaired assets from balance sheets and using those assets to create marketable securities may be an effective means of improving rates of collection and/or prices of substandard assets. The experience of the Resolution Trust Corporation in using securitisation to deal with widespread insolvency in the savings and loan industry in the United States may be highly significant in this connection. At this time, other OECD countries are considering the use of securitisation in dealing with similar problems.

Securitisation has some appeal for other market participants, as well as for financial intermediaries. Securitisation can offer non-financial companies a range of opportunities to obtain funding on more favourable terms than through bank loans, and to obtain better control over their balance sheets.

Overall, the incentives to engage in securitisation are strongest when the financial system is obliged to deal with increased volatility in interest rates, and/or when financial institutions are under pressure to improve capital adequacy ratios. Incentives are even stronger if some institutions have a serious overhang of impaired assets and/or if the system of housing finance is perceived to be deficient. Other things being equal, securitisation is likely to develop in countries where intermediation through the capital market is important. Conversely, the motivation for undertaking securitisation will be weak if banks and other credit institutions are well capitalised and if alternative means exist to manage maturity mismatches. Furthermore, the lack of a diverse base of domestic institutional investors will likely prove a disincentive. Thus, in several European countries where banks are sufficiently capitalised and where an adequate system of mortgage finance is present, securitisation has not made much headway. In any case, the experience of banks in the United States in improving the strength of their balance sheets by slowing the growth of lending, and indeed of all assets, is distinctive. Even in OECD countries where banks have difficulties with balance sheet quality, loan growth has consistently outpaced that of the United States since the mid-1980s.

An important precondition for securitisation is that the legal, accounting, tax and regulatory systems (characterised in this text as the "financial infrastructure" for securitisation) allow the transfer of assets to proceed with adequate protection for investors and in a cost-efficient manner. However, several of the common procedures in securitisation may come into conflict with long-standing legal, accounting and regulatory practice in some jurisdictions. In particular, those systems must permit the removal of assets from bank balance sheets and recognise the resulting security. Similarly, the tax system must not render securitisation uncompetitive with alternative financial operations which are economically similar. ABS and MBS must be recognised as securities by the securities regulators.

As recently as the early 1990s, the appropriate infrastructure was absent in most OECD countries. However, the authorities of several Member countries, convinced of the importance of securitisation as a technique of financial management, have taken or are in the process of taking measures to adapt domestic, legal, accounting and regulatory structures to foster its development. Experience has shown that this process is often quite long. Efforts to enable market participants to engage in securitisation frequently do not succeed on the first attempt, since it is usually very difficult to create an appropriate mechanism that meets the requirements of domestic lawyers and regulators while remaining sufficiently attractive to market participants.

In addition to its potential benefits, securitisation is sometimes perceived by financial executives and officials as having potentially undesirable consequences. Many financial officials believe that by diminishing the pivotal role of banks in financial intermediation, securitisation lessens the effectiveness of monetary policy. Banks and regulators in many countries are concerned that the weakening of close ties between banks and their corporate customers may undermine not only traditional patterns of financial intermediation, but patterns of corporate governance as well. The viability of certain categories of intermediary, especially those engaging in mortgage finance, and of instruments (*e.g.* mortgage bonds) can be threatened. Finally, efforts to accommodate the advance of securitisation through wide-ranging changes in domestic practices might have undesirable implications throughout domestic legal, tax accounting or regulatory systems. Thus, there does not appear to be a strong consensus among officials and financial analysts in OECD countries as to how far it is appropriate to modify domestic systems in order to encourage the development of off-balance-sheet securitisation.

Taking into account both the strength of demand on the part of market participants and the degree to which financial infrastructure favours securitisation, it is possible to make some broad categorisations of OECD countries. Counting the United States apart, they would fall into five groups:

i) In some countries, the existing financial infrastructure clearly permits securitisation. However, owing to lack of demand by market participants, activity remains on a relatively small scale. This category would include Australia, Canada, New Zealand, and the United Kingdom. In fact, Australia and Canada have official programmes to support housing finance that resemble US programmes, but in neither case has the mortgage-backed market attained anything like the proportions seen in the United States. There are no obvious impediments to securitisation in Denmark or the Netherlands, but no operations have yet been launched.

ii) In some countries, the authorities and/or major private institutions have seen advantages in the introduction of off-balance-sheet securitisation, and significant progress has been made in developing the appropriate framework. France, where some activity has already taken place, is a clear example. The category would also include Belgium, Finland and Spain. Sweden should soon also have an appropriate infrastructure in place. In most of these cases, however, actual activity is small or non-existent and prospects are uncertain. Similarly, in Japan, a number of measures have been adopted which make it possible to engage in securitisation on a limited scale. It should now be possible to launch MBS or ABS, although considerable effort is still required to comply with complex regulations, and the market in securitised assets will be available only to certain categories of financial institutions and institutional investors. The authorities will seek to ascertain the strength of market demand before considering further modifications in the legal and regulatory framework.

iii) In Germany there are no specific impediments to off-balance-sheet securitisation, and it is theoretically possible to remove assets from banks balance sheets via asset sales. Nevertheless, both banking supervisors and private market participants consider such practices to be inherently riskier than traditional on-balance sheet securitisation. Hence, requests to grant off-balance-sheet treatment to specific transactions are subjected to very careful scrutiny.

iv) In a number of countries, the regulatory framework contains provisions that clearly inhibit domestic securitisation. Austria would be in this category. Securitisation would also be difficult in Switzerland, where the authorities have not yet decided whether policies should be modified to allow it to proceed on a larger scale. In these cases, as well as in Germany, the demand for securitisation is also dampened by a strong universal banking system which traditionally has not relied heavily on capital markets for finance. Moreover, in all these countries, the strong balance sheets of the domestic banks and well-developed local mortgage finance systems further limit the motivation to pursue off-balance-sheet securitisation. In Norway, the domestic legal and institutional system is not conducive to securitisation, while the presence of a large number of specialised state banks to support particular activities, including housing, further discourages securitisation.

v) In a few cases, notably Italy, some measures have been taken to facilitate securitisation, but remaining ambiguities – particularly those concerning the legal status of asset-backed and mortgage-backed securities – are sufficiently important to pose a possible barrier to securitisation. In this case as well, the demand of issuers and investors remains uncertain.

In sum, the experience of OECD countries as a group suggests that, the lack of an appropriate "financial infrastructure" may be a partial explanation for the slow growth of securitisation outside the United States, but it is obviously not a full one. Indeed, even in cases where domestic regulations clearly permit securitisation, activity has to date been restrained; market participants have not yet sought to use the technique on a large scale.

The preceding discussion mainly concerned domestic securitisation. It is also worth mentioning that a considerable volume of cross-border securitisation is taking place, mainly in the form of sale of receivables to offshore SPVs. Securities created in this matter are marketed to the international investor community. Some cross-border securitisation is undertaken by institutions based in countries where domestic securitisation is relatively easy. At the same time, even when domestic infrastructure renders securitisation impractical, market participants have found cross-border activity to be a means of, engaging in securitisation. Thus, many non-financial companies in several countries have used offshore companies to issue ABS and MBS in cases where domestic systems made such operations impossible. Similarly, many banks have sponsored asset-backed commercial paper programmes in the United States or in the euro-markets, and such facilities are regularly used by the corporate customers of these banks. There is every reason to expect such practices to continue.

The question of whether securitisation will become an important feature of financial intermediation outside the United States remains unanswered. Some acceleration of growth could be observed in certain markets (*e.g.* France, Spain, and United Kingdom) in 1993-1994 while major advances were made in putting the proper infrastructure in place (*e.g.* in Belgium, France and Spain). Thus, many observers believe that the long-awaited international expansion of securitisation may occur in coming years.

It is at any rate possible to identify some countries where prospects for at least moderate expansion in the near term appear reasonably bright at this time. In countries where interest in these products is already strong and/or where a significant number of operations have already been launched the banks continue to experiment with securitisation partly in order to develop a full range of techniques which can be used on a broad scale if demand for this product increases. France, Spain and the United Kingdom are examples that can be mentioned in this context. Similarly, in Finland and Sweden, wherethe appropriate infrastructure is in place (or is likely to be in the near future) and the need to use bank capital efficiently is acute due to the financial crises of the early 1990s there is growing interest in securitisation. These countries also might find securitisation to be a useful means of dealing with impaired assets. In a few countries, MBS issuance could play an enlarged significant role in housing finance; the best prospects for expansion would appear to be in Finland, France, Spain, Sweden and the United Kingdom.

The remainder of this study is structured as follows. Chapter 2 reviews experience to date with securitisation and similar techniques in OECD countries. The main category of instrument that bears some resemblance to a MBS or ABS are mortgage bonds and communal bonds which are found in a number of European countries and used mainly for on-balance-sheet funding of assets. Next, off-balance-sheet securitisation is considered, first in the United States and then in other countries. Chapter 3 analyses the underlying economic and structural factors which might favour off-balance-sheet securitisation and the requirements for an appropriate financial infrastructure while describing some of the mechanisms used in securitisation. Chapter 4 highlights some issues for policymakers. Chapter 5 presents some tentative conclusions regarding the prospects for the international growth of securitisation. Chapter 6 presents a series of ''Country Notes'' summarising in some detail the situation in all OECD countries in which significant activity is found in securitisation or similar activities.

Chapter 2

HISTORICAL BACKGROUND

In international financial discourse, the term "securitisation" has been used in two different ways. In the early to mid-1980s, it denoted a general trend at the time in which sovereign entities or private corporations issued debt securities (bonds, commercial paper, medium-term notes, etc.) as relatively close substitutes for bank credit. The decision whether to purchase such securities reflected the investor's judgement of the credit standing of the borrower relative to the yield. At that time, many commercial banks viewed securitisation as representing a potential loss of business inasmuch as the increasing use of capital markets by large corporate borrowers appeared to remove one of the mainstays of traditional banking. This was particularly true in countries (such as the United States) which had traditions of banking/securities separation, for part of the revenue from lending which was lost to the commercial bank was reflected in increased fee income by an investment bank. (Admittedly, some opportunities were also created for "fee-based" activity by commercial banks.)

Since the mid-1980s, by contrast, "securitisation" has been used to describe operations in which the cash flows from specific assets are isolated from the balance sheet of the originating institution and used to support marketable securities. The banks have often been initiators of this process. This study will focus on the latter kind of securitisation in which the investor's decision is to a large degree separated from the credit standing of the institution which originates the assets and instead reflects an analysis of the underlying cash flows and of the various guarantees incorporated in the structure of the security.

Although securitisation in the second sense has only recently emerged as a significant trend in global finance, the creation and distribution of asset-related securities, especially mortgage bonds, has been practised for some time now in several European countries. This traditional system which can be classified as "on-balance-sheet securitisation", will be described below in Section A. In Section B, the experience in the United States will be discussed. The American model of off-balance-sheet securitisation, which was introduced in the euro-markets in the 1980s, has been the model most commonly used in countries seeking to develop domestic systems of securitisation. Thus, Section C will discuss the spread of securitisation to other OECD countries.

15

A. Traditional asset-related securities

Mortgage bonds and communal bonds in Europe

Several European countries have well-developed markets in asset-related bonds, most of which have been in existence for many decades. The most common assets supporting bonds are residential mortgages, but mortgages on industrial or agricultural land or equipment may also be used as security. Mortgage bond markets are found in Austria, Denmark, Finland, France, Germany, Italy, the Netherlands, Norway, Spain, Sweden and Switzerland.

A similarly important category of asset-related bond consists of "communal bonds" which are supported by receivables from local authorities and other public sector entities. By far the largest market in communal bonds is in Germany, but markets in these securities are also found in Austria, France and Italy.

Table 1 shows the outstanding volume of mortgage bonds and communal bonds in Europe. The total volume, some 800 billion ECU ($900 billion), dwarfs the outstanding amounts of ABS and MBS in all countries except the United States, and by a wide margin. It should be kept in mind that in addition to the issue of asset-related bonds by specialised institutions, universal banks in Europe also commonly participate in the bond market by purchasing asset-related bonds (mortgage bonds, communal bonds, ABS and MBS), as well as by issuing bonds for general funding purposes.

Table 1. **Mortgage bonds and communal bonds in European OECD countries**

(million ECU outstanding, end-1993)

Country	Mortgage bonds	Communal bonds	Total
Austria	4 892	9 086	13 978
Denmark	123 502	0	123 502
Finland	2 094	0	2 094
France	30 226	1 110	31 336
Germany	142 177	303 994	446 170
Greece	15	0	15
Italy	41 187	10 432	51 620
Luxembourg[a]	0	827	827
Netherlands	1 845	0	1 845
Norway	8 570	0	8 570
Portugal	28	0	28
Spain	6 310	0	6 310
Sweden	95 724	329	96 053
Switzerland	16 652	0	16 652
Total	473 221	325 779	799 000

a) Mainly bonds supported by receivables from local authorities in other countries.
Source: European Mortgage Federation.

Under the laws of the countries where such instruments are found, the asset-related securities may be issued only by specialised institutions which are often majority-owned subsidiaries of the commercial banks. Such specialised institutions engage in on-balance-sheet lending, usually for comparatively long periods at fixed rates. These institutions normally obtain funding not through deposits, but through issuance of mortgage bonds which enables long-term lending institutions to minimise the potential mismatch between the long-term assets in their portfolios and the short term maturities of most deposits. The issue of mortgage bonds is usually limited by requirements to observe property valuation and loan-to-value (LTV) ratios.

Since mortgage institutions engage in on-balance-sheet finance, investors in mortgage bonds hold a claim against the issuing institution rather than against specific assets of those institutions. However, in Denmark, Finland, Germany and Norway, the investor also has a special conditional claim on the cash flows from a specific pool of mortgages or similar collateral as additional security.

Although national markets in mortgage bonds share some characteristics, there are considerable differences. One of these relates to the importance of mortgage bonds in the financial system. In some cases, such as Denmark, Germany and Sweden, they are among the most significant capital market instruments, and are very important in overall housing finance. In Norway, such bonds are important capital market instruments but are not important in housing finance. In most other countries they are of lesser importance in both categories.

The degree to which mortgage finance is separate from the banking system also differs among countries. In Denmark, where the separation is most extreme, the involvement of banks in the mortgage bond market has traditionally been minimal, and the system of mortgage finance relies heavily on capital markets. The mortgage institutions, which have traditionally been independent of the commercial banks, specialise in originating mortgage bonds and selling those bonds to investors (insurance companies and pension funds). In most other cases, and notably Germany and Sweden, mortgage institutions are generally subsidiaries of banks while both banks and institutional investors purchase mortgage bonds. In Germany, mortgage bonds (as well as government and bank bonds) are purchased by banks and non-bank investors which use them partly to attain a desired maturity structure for their portfolios. The following paragraphs discuss some of the major markets in mortgage bonds and similar instruments, as well as related market structures.

In *Germany*, private mortgage banks (which in many cases are majority-owned subsidiaries of commercial banks) and public sector mortgage banks, as well as three "mixed" commercial banks, issue mortgage bonds (*Hypothekenpfandbriefe*) that are secured by mortgages on residential or commercial real estate which the institutions have taken as security. Maturities are usually from two to ten years, but some maturities are as long as fifty years. A similar asset is the communal bond (*Kommunalobligation*); mostly issued in the form of *Öffentliche Pfandbriefe*, these bonds are supported by receivables from public sector entities, such as local authorities, Länder governments, and Federal Government entities. Originally, communal bonds were just a supplementary business to the issue of mortgage bonds, but in recent years the latter have been dwarfed in relative importance by communal bonds. In addition, commercial banks as well as other special-ised financial institutions issue quite a number of bonds, domestically as well as abroad, for a multitude of purposes, including variable or fixed-rate mortgage lending for the financing of residential and commercial real estate. In these cases, the investor is not specifically protected by any possible direct recourse to any collateral.

In the case of mortgage bonds and communal bonds, the originating institution keeps the asset on its balance sheet and maintains ultimate responsibility for the credit risk of the bond, while the investor assumes all market risks. In effect, the investor is a senior creditor, with the underlying mortgage serving as collateral to guarantee payment of interest and principal. The investor also retains recourse to the issuing institution. The major holders of these assets are banks and retail investors. Insurance companies, invest-ment funds and non-financial corporations are also significant buyers, but pension funds are relatively small in Germany. These assets are treated favourably by the supervisory authorities, particularly those responsible for the investments of insurance companies. In recent years, non-resident institutional investors have started to show interest in mortgage and communal bonds which have low spreads over the yields of Federal Government bonds even though their liquidity is considerably less.

This market offers attractions to all participants. For all investors, mortgage bonds and communal bonds offer the possibility to obtain a higher yield than is available on government bonds while minimising credit risk by allowing them to become secured senior creditors of a major financial institution. These bonds also offer the possibility for the institutional investor to acquire assets that, from the maturity viewpoint, match liabilities.

In effect, this form of on-balance-sheet securitisation results in banks "unbundling" the credit risks, which are retained, from the market risks inherent in long-term fixed rate assets, and passing the market risks on to investors. To the degree that institutions mainly depend upon short-term deposits for funding and have longer-term assets in their portfo-lios, the risk of maturity mismatches can be serious. Alternatively, banks seeking longer term assets at fixed interest rates can purchase mortgage bonds and expand their balance sheets or reshape their maturity profiles. Since the larger German banks, as already mentioned, are also among the major issuers of bonds that are used for funding, they can act on both sides of the market (*i.e.* as issuers and investors), thereby controlling the size of their balance sheets as well as the maturity structure of their assets and liabilities. In effect, the German banks were able to achieve many of the benefits that are now provided by derivatives well before the use of such instruments became common. In more recent times, the use of swaps has made it possible to add even greater flexibility to this market.

Because the banks are heavily involved in all phases of the asset-related securities market, the German system does not imply the high degree of disintermediation (*i.e.* a declining share of conventional bank lending in total intermediation) that characterised some recently developed markets in securitised assets. Thus, this market has enabled the German system of financial intermediation – which remains heavily dominated by univer-sal banks – to gain considerable flexibility and liquidity. At the same time, since the originating institution retains full responsibility for the credit risk of the assets, any loss in the credit standing of the originator would have a direct impact on the prices and marketability of assets.

In *Denmark*, the mortgage finance system has traditionally relied more heavily on the capital market than in any country in Europe, and the involvement of banks has been minimal. Danish banks have historically not been major originators of residential mortgages. Instead, specialised mortgage institutions, which have been mutual associations traditionally independent of the commercial banks, are funded by the issue of securities based upon pools of residential or commercial mortgages. These institutions retain mortgages on their books and act as guarantors, with the capital of the institution serving as the guarantor of the loan in the first instance. Borrowers have joint and several responsibility within limits for the payments of principal and interest on loans in their own pool, which provides a second guarantee. The main investors are pension funds and other institutions which tend to hold longer-dated assets to match liabilities. Banks and foreign investors each hold about 10 per cent of the total.

Despite the country's small size, the fixed-income market is rather large and liquid, and major efforts have been made in the past few years to upgrade trading and reporting practices, which are now of very high quality. With relatively few other possibilities, government and mortgage bonds were traditionally the only investments available on a large scale to Danish institutions. The corporate bond sector and the domestic equity markets are not very well developed. In the past, Denmark had explicit limitations on foreign investment. Exchange controls have now been eliminated, but prudential measures now still restrain foreign investment.

In the past decade, the Danish mortgage system has undergone structural change, which has brought Danish practice closer to those in other major European markets. Most mortgage institutions now function as parts of bank-affiliated financial groups. In keeping with EC capital adequacy directives, the joint and several responsibility of borrowers will be phased out before the year 2000.

In *Sweden*, housing finance is typically provided by special mortgage institutions, most of which are subsidiaries of banks. These institutions obtain funding by issuing mortgage bonds, mostly in "bullet" form, with maturities of two or five years. Mortgage bonds account for some two-thirds of total outstanding bonds in the country. The main purchasers are Swedish institutional investors such as the National Pension Fund and insurance companies; foreign investors also hold a moderate share.

In *Norway*, mortgage bonds are a major financial instrument but are not widely used for housing finance.

In a few countries, mortgage bonds are of only moderate importance. In *Switzerland*, for example, mortgages are mainly provided by the commercial banks. Under certain conditions, all commercial banks have access to specialised mortgage institutions which issue mortgage bonds; these bonds account for 5 to 10 per cent of total mortgages and 15 per cent of the total domestic bond market. Since mortgages are fixed-rate and medium to long-term, Swiss commercial banks have become more concerned about interest rate risk, especially in view of increased volatility of recent years. As banks have been able to deal with these problems adequately to date, mortgage bonds still only play a secondary role as risk management instruments. In *France*, a large share of mortgages are provided by the banks under special programmes which have government subsidies of various kinds. Nevertheless, a mortgage bond market does exist. Mortgage bonds, which may only be issued by two specialised institutions, account for 6 per cent of total mortgages and 16 per cent of domestic bonds. A system of mortgage finance is also that found in *Italy*, where mortgages are usually provided by specialised credit institutions, are mostly owned by banks. These institutions fund themselves through the issuance of mortgage bonds. However, mortgages are granted for a comparatively small share of assessed property value, and cash purchases have been fairly common.

There are a number of countries in which mortgage bonds do exist but are not a major financial instrument. In the *Netherlands*, a market in mortgage bonds is found but it has remained comparatively small. Under Dutch law it is not possible to use specific loans to collateralise mortgage-related securities, and hence the investor does not obtain a credit enhancement. In effect, the investor always carries an unsecured claim against the issuing bank. Nevertheless, since the investor assumes market risk, the Dutch mortgage bond market has the capacity to transform the term structure of assets and to minimise maturity mismatches. However, specialised mortgage institutions are not an important provider of mortgage finance, and mortgage bonds have no special attraction for investors in comparison to ordinary bank bonds, which are a much more significant funding vehicle. In *Finland*, the banks have traditionally been the main providers of housing finance. However, in recent times, an increasing share of mortgages have been granted by special mortgage subsidiaries of the major banks, which issue bonds secured by receipts from mortgages.

In *Spain*, the authorities made considerable efforts to develop a conventional market in mortgage-related securities in the early 1980s, but the market did not attain large proportions. Partly as a result, greater consideration has been given recently to the expanded use of off-balance-sheet securitisation.

Other asset-related securities

In some OECD countries, other forms of secured bonds are issued. For example, in *Australia*, some finance companies issue medium-term bonds (debentures) which are secured by charges against the assets of the issuer. Assets to support these securities typically include consumer, automobile, finance lease and property receivables. In addition to the collateral, the issue of debentures are also supported by the covenants restricting the total level of debentures to a specified portion of an asset category (*e.g.* loans and advances) or limits on balance sheet gearing. Finance company debentures outstanding in June 1994 amounted to A\$ 10 billion. The major issuers are finance company subsidiaries of the major banks or specialised finance subsidiaries of automobile companies.

Another asset-related instrument that is found in Australia is the retail mortgage trust; which collects savings from small and medium investors and invests in liquid assets and medium term loans secured against mortgages over property. Investments can generally be redeemed at relatively short notice (*e.g.* 21 days). Some of these trusts are listed on the stock exchange. Mortgage trusts do not constitute an important part of the financial system, with only A\$ 2 billion outstanding in March 1994.

In the *United States*, some Federal housing agencies issue corporate bonds that are used for funding mortgages held by the agency. However, these bonds have remained of marginal significance, while the MBS market has enjoyed tremendous growth.

Observations

In most OECD countries, mortgage bonds have functioned as part of closed national systems of financial intermediation which involved a heavy degree of official regulation. (This can be contrasted to the situation in the United States, where most innovative products have been developed by the private institutions, and where experimentation is constant. The infrastructure that favoured the development of corporate debt markets in the United States – *i.e.* a deep institutional investor community, rating agencies, and a powerful securities market supervisor enforcing strong disclosure requirements and monitoring trading practices has been largely absent.) Most corporate borrowers have relied on loans from banks, while a small number of well-known larger private companies made offshore bond issues. In countries with mortgage bond markets, laws have stipulated that only specified kinds of institutions could engage in mortgage finance, and these were usually the only institutions permitted to issue mortgage bonds. Similarly, regulations governing the portfolios of institutional investors, especially pension funds and insurance companies, strongly favoured investments in these assets. In any event, given the narrow range of domestic bonds (which usually included only government, mortgage and possibly bank-issued bonds), the range of choice for domestic institutions was limited.

In the past, investors were often further constrained in their choice due to exchange controls. With the liberalisation of controls in the 1980s, such constraints have become less significant. At the same time, prudential regulations on institutions' portfolio allocations continue to restrain domestic institutions' portfolio allocation decisions. Ceilings may be placed on investments in foreign securities or bonds in foreign currency, thus effectively limiting investors to a narrow range of domestic assets.

The process of financial modernisation may eventually encourage convergence of traditional mortgage bond systems with international practice. With the deregulation of domestic securities markets and the easing of controls on cross-border operations, investment banks will create debt instruments that improve yield while using risk management techniques (especially derivatives) to enable investors to manage currency risk more effectively. Similarly, EC rules regarding large exposures may oblige investors to lessen concentration of investments in a small number of domestic issuers. Some mortgage institutions have also shown interest in using MBS issuance to supplement traditional mortgage bonds.

Possibly in recognition of the need to respond to increased deregulation and internationalisation of bond markets, some issuers of traditional mortgage bonds have been trying to interest international investors in domestic mortgage bonds. In this respect, it is noteworthy that German mortgage banks are seeking to inform international investors of the attractions of holding the *Pfandbrief* in an international portfolio. Likewise, some international investors have reportedly been interested in purchasing mortgage bonds in countries such as Denmark and Sweden.

In general, the existence of advanced markets in mortgage bonds tends to slow the introduction of newer types of off-balance-sheet securitisation, particularly mortgage-backed securities. Such instruments enable credit institutions to obtain many of the benefits of off-balance-sheet securitisation, thus obviating the need for those techniques.

Incentives to resort to off-balance-sheet securitisation will be further weakened when domestic banks and specialised mortgage institutions are well capitalised. Thus, in countries such as Austria, Germany and Switzerland – where universal banks have traditionally dominated all facets of financial intermediation and where the banks have remained strong – interest in pursuing off-balance-sheet securitisation has not been great. Similarly, when much of the population is able to obtain fixed-rate mortgage finance at reasonable cost, the existing system of mortgage finance will generally be broadly supported by the public as well as by financial supervisors and legislators. The authorities may be very reluctant to modify domestic legal accounting and prudential practices -- which may be closely tied to socially satisfactory patterns of domestic finance, particularly where domestic financial institutions are seen as sound.

On the other hand, where the domestic mortgage bond system is not a major source of housing finance and/or where some credit institutions are not financially strong, both the institutions themselves and the authorities are likely to be more favourably disposed to consider the case for newer forms of securitisation. This technique may be useful where banks and supervisors are seeking either to improve capital adequacy by downsizing balance sheets or to dispose of impaired assets.

B.   Securitisation in the United States

Over the past two decades, securitisation has emerged as a distinctive feature of the financial system in the United States. To some degree this reflects the fact that the United States has long had two channels for financial intermediation (the banking system and the capital market), with the competitive balance between the two channels often changing over time. In recent years in particular, the process of disintermediation by the banking system has progressed farther than in other OECD countries, and to some degree securitisation is one manifestation of this broader process. There is some controversy as to whether the process of "disintermediation" represents a declining role for banks in financial intermediation, or merely a shift by banks to off-balance-sheet activity. In either case, the analysis presented here would not be affected.[1]

American-style securitisation has typically involved complete removal of the securitised asset from the balance sheet of the originating institution. The assets become "collateral" which supports the payments of interest and principal on the newly created security. If the originating institution continues to participate, it is usually as "servicer", *i.e.* the collector of principal and interest payments and processor of other back-office functions related to the assets supporting the transaction. The collateral which produces the cash flows to support the security are segregated into an identifiable pool. The investor purchases a security which is based upon the cash flows resulting from the securitised assets *without* recourse to the originating institution, and thus accepts all risks inherent in the assets, including credit, market and prepayment risk. Indeed, this is a test that is usually applied by accountants, lawyers, rating agencies and regulators: have all risks associated with a given asset in fact been transferred from the originator?

Mortgage-backed securities

The largest category of instrument created by securitisation are MBS supported by United States Government agencies or Federally-sponsored companies and fall into the broad category of "government agency paper" – a category of assets considered fairly close to Treasury securities in terms of credit risk, but with somewhat higher yields. At the end of 1993 the outstanding stock of US agency MBS exceeded $1.7 trillion and represented the second largest category of bonds in the United States after Treasury bonds. Historically, the United States housing market has been characterised by long-term fixed-rate mortgages, with 30 years often the norm. Traditionally, mortgage finance was provided by depository institutions, *i.e.* banks and savings and loan association (or "thrifts"). MBS issuance, which began in the early 1970s, was spurred by two important developments. First, increased interest rate volatility heightened the risk of maturity mismatches. Second, programmes were begun under which Federal agencies guaranteed residential mortgages for fees and used the mortgages as collateral to support securities which were sold to investors.

Three institutions are responsible for most mortgage-backed securitisation: the Government National Mortgage Association (GNMA), which is a Federal agency; and the Federal Home Loan Mortgage Corporation (FHLMC) and Federal National Mortgage Association (FNMA), which are government-sponsored enterprises. The agencies may purchase these mortgages from the originating depository institutions (banks or thrifts), thereby removing them from the balance sheets of the originators. MBS can also be originated by mortgage companies, a newer form of institution which specialises in mortgage origination for off-balance-sheet operations. Usually, the originating institution continues as "servicer" of the underlying loans. Some 55-60 per cent of total United States residential mortgages are now securitised.

The simplest MBS is a "pass-through" security, which merely receives the funds paid to the servicer and transfers (or passes through) payments to investors. Because payments on these securities reflect the cash flows from mortgages, the flows are significantly different from those on Treasuries – although the credit risk is considered similar. Principal as well as interest payments will be repaid over the life of the loan, with principal repayments normally accelerating over time. Moreover, since mortgages usually allow borrowers to prepay, there is considerable risk of prepayment.

Much of the innovation in the MBS market has involved efforts to manage and to price prepayment risk. A major innovation in mortgage-backed financing was the development of Collateralised Mortgage Obligations (CMOs), first introduced in 1983, which gave investors an improved capacity to deal with the prepayment risk of pass-throughs. In the CMO market, pass-throughs are used as collateral to support "multi-class securities", in which investors are grouped into a number of classes which receive payment in a predetermined order. In the early days of the CMO market, it was common to group these cash flows into different (A, B, C and Z) "sequential pay" tranches. All payments of principal (including prepayments) are initially directed to the A tranche and successively to the B and C tranches. The Z tranche receives no payment until all earlier tranches are fully repaid.

The CMO structure enabled the investment community to restructure cash flows in intricate ways so as to match the maturity, liquidity and risk preferences of investors. The A tranche would often have an expected average life of one to three years while the Z tranche would have an expected average life of fifteen to twenty years. Given the highly diversified group of investors in the United States, the varying repayment profiles allow a variety of investors to choose a maturity position among the tranches. Other transformations of cash flows can be made, such as converting monthly receipts into quarterly payments, or creating interest-only or principal-only tranches. Many CMOs contain fixed as well as floating tranches. The great majority of pass-throughs are now transformed using the CMO mechanism. It was mentioned that CMOs originally contained four tranches, but in the late 1980s and early 1990s the number and complexity of tranches increased sharply. By 1993, some CMOs were issued with more than 100 tranches.

The turbulence in bond markets in the course of 1994 affected the MBS market in several ways. As interest rates began to rise in late 1993 and continued rising but at an unexpectedly rapid pace in 1994, a decline in the rate of mortgage refinancing ensued, thus reducing the amount of total MBS origination. Moreover, unlike most debt securities which have fixed durations, the duration of most MBS is a function of the interest rate; it tends to increase as interest rates rise. The lengthening duration of outstanding MBS has lengthened the duration of all portfolios containing MBS. This has obliged investors to take offsetting action (either sales of other bonds or activities in the derivatives market) to achieve their desired portfolio duration. Such activity was particularly intense in 1994, since investors' desired duration shortened as interest rates rose unexpectedly rapidly and as interest rate volatility increased. As a result of these developments, demand for complex tranches of CMOs has declined considerably, and many "exotic" tranches have become illiquid. Thus, in 1994 new CMO offerings tended toward fewer tranches and simpler structures.

So far, the discussion has only covered MBS with government guarantees or at least with strong government support, and hence the question of credit risk was not considered important. Eventually, however, a large number of "private label CMOs" (*i.e.* those without the support of a Federal agency) were issued. Originators of private label CMOs include banks, thrifts and home builders. Consequently, the question of credit risk became serious. Since the investor in a mortgage-backed security has no recourse to the originator, it is important to be sure that: *i)* the receivables are sufficient to generate the payments stipulated in the security; *ii)* some safeguards are provided in case of shortfalls in revenue; and *iii)* the investor has a sufficiently clear legal claim on income from the receivables and has adequate protection in case of delinquency. In order to assess and reduce credit risk, two major techniques were developed that have now come to characterise not only the US market, but the entire international market in MBS and ABS, namely *a)* the use of "credit enhancements" and *b)* a greatly enlarged role for the rating agencies.

Credit enhancements

Concerning the innovation of credit enhancements, the investor seeks not only assurance of repayment by examining risks inherent in the underlying cash flows, but also additional support. Credit enhancements can take several forms:

  i) Third party enhancement – An external party, often an insurance company or a bank, provides a guarantee. A number of specialised companies called "monoline insurers" have emerged; their sole function is to offer credit enhancements for fees. The guarantee can be for 100 per cent of payments (called "wraparound") or for some lesser amount.

  ii) Subordination – An alternative means of obtaining credit enhancement is to create a "senior/subordinated" structure, meaning that some creditors agree to grant priority to other (*i.e.* senior) creditors in case of difficulties in payment in exchange for different rates of return. One possible structure is for the "originator" to retain a subordinated tranche, but such structures create legal and regulatory questions as to whether a "true sale" of the asset has occurred, and assets securitised in this way may not qualify for off-balance-sheet treatment. In the United States, depository institutions do not normally retain subordinated tranches of receivables they originate. Subordinated tranches will often be assigned lower credit ratings than senior tranches. In some cases, subordinated tranches of securities can be privately placed while the senior tranches are publicly offered.

  iii) Overcollateralisation – The assets put into the pool can be of greater value than is needed to support the contractual payments, so that the investor is protected in the event of a shortfall in expected payments. The excess collateral is usually held in a subordinated tranche or a special account.

  iv) Cash collateral accounts – A cash deposit can be held in a special account which will allow for payments in case of shortfall of cash from the receivables. A slight variation is the "spread account", which represents the difference between the margin received by the originator and that of the investor: the originator will receive payment from the spread account only if other creditors are paid in full. Usually either cash collateral or spread accounts can be used in conjunction with a senior/subordinated structure.

Credit rating agencies

A central role has devolved to the credit rating agencies. Prior to issue, each security is examined by one or more rating agencies. The agencies only provide ratings of credit risk, so that the investor must devise other methods of assessing other risks, such as interest rate, exchange rate, volatility or prepayment risk. Since "structured financings" cannot be assessed on the strength of the originating institution's credit ratings, each security's ratings must be made on the basis of the risk in the cash flows, the collateral, and the enhancements. Moreover, since many of these financings are done in several tranches with varying degrees of seniority, different tranches of the same facility will often be assigned different credit ratings.

The rating agency will examine the historical performance of the receivables and will subject them to various "stress tests". Thus, the historical rates of delinquency on mortgages will be analysed and simulations will be made to identify the most unfavourable period for which records exist, for example rates of mortgage delinquency in the Depression of the 1930s or the sharpest declines in property prices recorded in the twentieth century. On this basis, the agency will indicate the amount of credit enhancement that is needed to achieve a desired rating. Negotiations can take place between the investment bankers and rating agencies concerning hypothetical structures and rating. For instance, it could be decided that based upon historical experience, the receivables are 95 per cent sufficient to cover contractual payments, and an external enhancement of 5 per cent will be needed to obtain a desired rating. Alternatively, it could be decided that a structure of 90 per cent senior debt and 10 per cent subordinated debt is required for the senior tranche to obtain a AAA rating.

The rating agency will usually perform further analysis. If any transformation of payments is involved, it will also need to determine whether internal mechanisms are adequate – for example, if a transformation from monthly to quarterly payments or prepayment risk is sufficiently covered by swaps and/or cash accounts. The agency will also examine whether the servicer has information systems in place to track payments accurately and to identify and report delinquencies in an acceptable manner, as well as to deal with delinquent payments. Methods for dealing with possible delinquency must be examined in advance.

The rating agency also examines external enhancements and usually applies the "weak link" principle, meaning that the rating of a security can be no higher than the rating of an external provider of enhancements. Thus, if a security depends upon an enhancement from an institution rated AA, the security can be rated no better than AA. As a result, a number of securities have been downgraded when an external provider of enhancements has been downgraded. The downgrading of other guarantors (particularly banks and insurance companies) has tended to strengthen the relative position of the "monoline insurers", who are all rated AAA, as well as other forms of enhancement.

In addition to examining the adequacy of cash flows and credit enhancements, the agencies seek to assure that the legal structure of the security affords adequate protection to investors. For example, in case of delinquency on receivables, the position of the investor with regard to other creditors must be clear and sufficiently strong to assure contractual payments. Due to their strong repayment histories and credit enhancements, the senior tranches of nearly all CMOs are rated either AAA or AA.

Asset-backed securities

In view of the success of the MBS market, market participants began experimenting with the securitisation of other assets. Assets that are easiest to securitise are those that occur in large pools for which past experience can be used to predict default rates and in which documentation is standardized, with the possibility of transfer claims. The most widely used collateral for ABS are credit card receivables, automobile loans, commercial

mortgages (single property and "pools"), leases and home equity loans. In mid-1994 the outstanding volume of publicly traded ABS in the United States was estimated at some $200 billion.

In most of the operations described thus far, the originator is a bank or other depository institution. By lowering the stock of assets while leaving capital unchanged, the capital/asset ratio of the originating institution is strengthened. Reducing assets can also be an efficient way to bring capital/assets ratios within regulatory norms. At the same time, the originator can continue to obtain earnings from the collateral by acting as a servicer. Moreover, the originating bank still can earn significant revenue on the interest margin from an asset that has been sold. Thus, earnings on collateral such as credit card receivables may exceed costs of funding by a wide margin. Even if part of this margin is passed on to investors, the remainder is earned by the originator. Thus, many banks have often found that they can increase their earnings on any given level of capital by securitising assets.

The examples cited thus far have involved depository institutions selling receivables to create an ABS. However, it is possible to create ABS originated by other kinds of institutions. Thus, non-bank financial companies (*e.g.* finance or leasing companies) can sell receivables directly to SPVs, as can banks. Non-financial companies can also utilise this technique. For example, retailers are a group of institutions with a kind of collateral that is rather easy to use in creating ABS. Similarly, trade receivables or lease receivables can be used to back securities. Although the receivables in question do not appear on a bank balance sheet, banks are often sponsors of these facilities and often participate by offering credit enhancements and/or liquidity facilities which allow them to earn fees without any capital charge. While the need to economise on capital is normally less of a motivation for non-bank originators than for banks, an ABS issue may be a cheaper means of raising funds than straight corporate debt. In particular, companies with relatively low ratings can use high-quality receivables to issue relatively well-rated securities.

One of the major innovations of the past few years has been the development of asset-backed commercial paper. Indeed, this product accounts for all net growth in the commercial paper (CP) market of the United States since 1986. Under an asset-backed CP programme, receivables from some commercial activity (for example credit card receivables) stand as support to a CP facility, under which borrowers can have direct access to investors for short-term funding, usually for no more than 270 days and with average lives of less than 90 days. They are placed in a facility which may contain receivables from more than one originator or from a single originator. Normally, new receivables enter the facility and other receivables mature continually.

Although the issue of ABS (including asset-backed CP) that is originated by non-financial institutions can be seen as an instance of the banks' declining role in financial intermediation and a rise in the role of the capital market, it is also a development in which the banks have taken a leading role. In fact, banks were among the most aggressive institutions in developing the market in ABS using credit card receivables as collateral. Similarly, banks have been important in promoting asset-backed CP. More than half of all asset-backed CP programmes and about 80 per cent of asset-backed CP outstandings in the United States are bank-advised. Many banks see the issue of ABS as an effective means of earning fees while conserving capital. Banks also participate in asset-backed CP programmes by offering credit enhancements (usually in the form of letters of credit which may be for all or part of contractual payments) or liquidity facilities. In many instances, banks advise their corporate customers to use an asset-backed CP programme rather than a bank loan as the most effective means of funding. Thus, the growth of the asset-backed CP market is both 1) an instance of disintermediation (meaning a replacement of bank lending by the direct recourse of borrowers to the capital market), and 2) a shift in banks to off-balance-sheet activity as a means of increasing earnings, managing risk and utilising bank more efficiently.

The capacity of the investment community in the United States to construct new instruments appears limitless. The discussion thus far has mainly emphasized the more commonly used forms of collateral, such as residential mortgages, consumer loans, credit card receivables, trade receivables, etc. However, many in the financial services community believe that a large untapped potential exists to create securities based on other forms of collateral. At this time, intermediaries are trying to securitise commercial mortgages and commercial loans. Consideration is also being given to the securitisation of small business loans. Despite the problems in securitising some kinds of assets, many analysts are convinced that ultimately, most categories of bank loans can be securitised.

Another major category of securitisation activity is known as "repackaging"; in this case a security is created by purchasing an existing pool of securities or of loans and restructuring them so as to alter the payments and/or credit rating by adding seniority provisions or other credit enhancements. In some senses, the simplest repackaging operation is the "stripping" of Treasury securities: an investment bank purchases Treasuries and sells the principal and interest payments to different investors. The CMO market also engages in the repackaging of cash flows in government-backed MBS. In addition, the swap market may be used to transform some of the characteristics of the assets, such as transforming fixed-rate debt into floating-rate debt or swapping among currencies. (Such operations can be significant in helping investors who are subject to limits on currency or interest-rate exposure to achieve diversification while observing prudential limits.) In addition to transforming cash flows, repackaging can be used to modify credit risk and to create multiclass securities with different degrees of credit risk assumed by different investors. In particular, senior-subordinated structures can be created for a pool of assets and/or third-party enhancements can be used.

Structured finance operations known as collateralised loan obligations and collateralised bond obligations consist of pools of speculative-grade loans or bonds. The debt of developing countries is often "repackaged" in this way; thus, investment banks have discovered "excess collateralisation" in "Brady" bonds and resold the resulting cash flows. Cash flows can be divided into a number of tranches with various degrees of seniority. All of the techniques developed in the MBS market to transform payments structures and credit risk can be used in repackaging. For example, securities can be repackaged using currency swaps to meet the needs of investors seeking assets in a given currency.

Securitisation of impaired assets

A major extension of the application of securitisation has been the activity of the Resolution Trust Company (RTC) formed in 1989 to deal with the problem of insolvent savings and loan institutions ("S&Ls" or "thrifts"). After using a variety of techniques to dispose of failed institutions, including sales of entire institutions and of individual securities (ranging from Treasury paper to "junk bonds"), other assets were sold in "whole loan" form, *i.e.* without conversion to a security or through a programme of "bulk sales" in which investors were offered "pools" of assets (usually real estate), some of which was performing and some non-performing, at estimated market value. The purchaser was often an investment bank or an investor who wanted to acquire managerial control over the asset, or a combination of these. At the same time, the RTC found that many of the assets sold by either of these methods were eventually securitised by "repackaging" operations undertaken by the purchasers.

After April 1992, direct securitisation became the RTC's preferred method for disposing of assets. Some mortgages were eligible for inclusion in GNMA and FNMA pools, but the largest share of assets were sold under RTC "private label" CMOs for single-family mortgages. These securities received credit enhancement from subordination and overcollateralisation and through reserve funds which the RTC was pledged to maintain, provided losses remained below certain levels. Consumer receivables were also relatively easy to securitise. A number of somewhat more difficult claims were eventually securitised in large numbers, including single-family mortgages with high delinquency rates and pools of multi-unit residential mortgages. Most RTC securitisations of this kind have been rated AA or AAA.

Having disposed of easily saleable assets in this manner, it was necessary to turn to assets that were progressively harder to sell. In doing so, the RTC encountered problems similar to those that have hampered the securitisation of commercial mortgages, including the large size of individual loans, highly specific terms which limit homogeneity and transferability, problems in developing statistically credible payment histories, and difficulties in obtaining acceptable diversification. Nevertheless, the RTC was able to securitise pools of commercial mortgages with enhancement. The different tranches of these securities have been rated from AAA (the highest rating) to BBB (the lowest investment grade rating). Some have been done at fixed rates, and others at floating rates.

The RTC had to sell still less liquid assets. There was a large amount of non-performing or "underperforming" mortgages which required foreclosure and/or renegotiations of terms, as well as real estate directly owned by the RTC as a result of foreclosures which were consolidated in "structured transactions". The property is sold at an estimated market value (but below book value) and the investor assumes control in return for an asset with potential for appreciation, provided that the assets are managed properly. While the senior tranches, which were rated AA or AAA, were widely distributed, the "hard to sell" assets, particularly the subordinated tranches, were mainly sold to single investors who wished to maintain control over the properties.

The techniques developed by the RTC in liquidating failed thrifts may have wider applicability. It was possible to sell large amounts of assets, many of which were not easily marketable, in a comparatively short time. Many observers believe the prices received through securitisation compared favourably with those received from alternative methods. By selling assets relatively quickly, the need for Federal support was limited. At the same time, the RTC retains a large interest in the reserve funds, as well as equity positions in the subordinated tranches. Many agreements with their subordinated investors provide for a sharing of any gains on sale of the assets. Many of the deals were structured so as to provide investors with managerial control and strong incentives to maximise rates of recovery on assets.

Concluding remarks

The ABS and MBS markets have shown remarkable adaptability. The techniques developed in the United States have enabled financial institutions to create securities supported by a growing range of assets, and to enhance the control that investors and financial institutions exert over both cash flows attached to assets and credit risks.

It is arguable that since financing operations are scrutinised continuously by several parties (originators, investment banks, rating agencies, dealers and investors), risks tend to become increasingly transparent and pricing tends to be more efficient. Moreover, securitisation, along with other risk management techniques (especially derivatives and the application of portfolio theory), enables financial intermediaries and investors to manage risk more efficiently, and thus specialise in those activities they do best while assuming those risks they can best manage. Similarly, investors have another powerful tool to assist in the management of their own portfolios and the associated risks. In addition, there is a convincing argument that, since much risk is passed from banks – which are leveraged investors with access to official "safety nets" – to final investors who do not have access to safety rates, the level of systemic risk is reduced.

In some quarters, concern has been expressed about the dangers of erosion of relations between banks and their corporate and retail customers. Concerning one category of borrower – individuals seeking housing finance – it seems safe to say that the growth of the MBS market has clearly enlarged the possibilities for individuals to control borrowing conditions, since borrowers can choose between fixed and variable rate mortgages and have numerous options to prepay. In all likelihood, the financing costs for residential mortgages are no higher (and are almost certainly lower) than they would be without the MBS market. Despite the fact that securitisation has existed for more than two decades and through a number of cycles in the real estate market and interest rates, there is no evidence that individuals seeking housing finance have suffered in any way.

Regarding corporate borrowers, it is hard to argue that any serious damage has been inflicted by the growth of the ABS market. The displacement of bank lending by various forms of capital market operations has been a major trend in the financial market for more than a decade, a development largely prompted by corporations seeking to lower borrowing costs.

Several factors have encouraged the growth of securitisation in its various forms in the United States. Support from the Federal Government was very important in the early development of the MBS market. The large number of geographically dispersed banks may have given rise to a need for mechanisms to ease flows of resources among regions and reduce geographic risk concentration. The tradition of fixed-rate mortgages and the resulting risk of large asset/liability mismatches no doubt favoured securitisation. The separation between banking and securities has meant that there are alternative channels for financial intermediation; this can be contrasted to systems in which the commercial banks dominate most aspects of financial intermediation. It should be emphasized that, even in the case of the US financial system where there is significant competition between banks and other financial institutions, the shift of intermediation from on-balance-sheet bank lending to capital market activities does not necessarily exclude banks from participation in the intermediation process. Banks have shown considerable adaptability in moving from lending to off-balance-sheet fee-based business. Indeed, the very slow expansion of bank balance sheets in general and of bank lending in particular between the mid-1980s and early 1990s is the one clearest instances of divergence between banks in the United States and those in other OECD countries.

Other important trends in the US financial system probably further encouraged securitisation. Different classes of institutions (banks, thrift institutions, securities houses, institutional investors) often compete among themselves in devising new products. An institutionalisation of wealth has been occurring in the United States, creating a large and diverse community of institutional investors and an attendant demand for securities with different liquidity and maturity preferences, and allowing a distribution of securities with multiple tranches throughout the community. Finally, the legal, accounting, and tax systems as well as the banking and securities supervisory authorities have generally been willing to accept securitisation.

C. The international expansion of securitisation

Since the mid-1980s, the techniques of "American style" off-balance-sheet securitisation have begun to be introduced into an increasing number of national markets. As with many other forms of financial innovation, the pattern of transference has been for techniques first perfected in the United States to be introduced in the euro-markets and thence in other national markets. After observing the relevance of these techniques for problems facing financial institutions, private institutions in many countries have begun to experiment with securitisation. Meanwhile, the authorities of several OECD countries have recognised the potential uses of securitisation in their own financial systems and thus have sought to adapt their financial systems in order to facilitate its development. By and large, the promotion of fixed-rate mortgage finance has not been the primary motivation for securitisation. Rather, private financial institutions and officials have been more interested in promoting securitisation for other purposes, particularly removing assets from the balance sheets of originators and thereby improving the capacity of banks to gain better control over the risk/return profile of their balance sheets. With the imposition of tougher capital adequacy rules, the objective of using bank capital more efficiently has become more explicit, especially in cases where capital/asset ratios are near (or below) international norms. This section will present an overview of the progress of securitisation outside the United States.

The largest market in securitised assets in Europe, and the second largest in the world, is in the *United Kingdom.* At the end of 1994, total MBS outstanding were estimated at about £16 billion, while ABS totalled about £3 billion. By way of comparison, the size of the MBS market in the United States other than those based on Federal agency paper was of the order of $130 billion, and asset-backed securities amounted to about $200 billion. The largest volume of structured financings in the United Kingdom has been in the form of variable-rate MBS. However, only about 3 per cent of residential mortgages have been securitised in the United Kingdom, compared with 50-60 per cent in the United States.

Most housing finance has traditionally been done by building societies and banks, both of which generally keep mortgages on their books. In the 1980s, Specialist Mortgage Lenders (SMLs), which are companies designed to originate mortgages using off-balance-sheet securitisation, began to operate.

The MBS market expanded rapidly after the first deals in 1985-1986, but reached a peak in 1988. The SMLs originated most MBS, with commercial banks also issuing small amounts. Subsequently, the depressed prices of houses have eroded the base of security for investors. The reduction in credit ratings of several banks and insurers has led to the downgrading of the securities for which they had provided enhancements. Other events also weakened confidence in the sector. National Home Loans (NHL) Company, an SML, underwent financial difficulties. (Nevertheless, securities originated by National Home Loan Company continued to perform well, proving the ''bankruptcy remote'' nature of the securities and NHL continued to issue in 1994.) Finally, the market was negatively affected by concerns that the banking supervisory authorities would assign a 100 per cent risk weighting to mortgage-backed securities, rather than a 50 per cent weighting. In fact, the main purchasers of MBS have been banks and building societies, with only a small amount of paper actually being placed with institutional investors.

The ABS market, which began in 1990 with an issue supported by automobile loans, is considerably smaller than the MBS market. At the end of 1994, total outstandings were about £3 billion. Collateral for ABS included leases, auto receivables, swap receivables, personal loans and impaired assets.

The main explanation of the slow growth of securitisation in the United Kingdom apparently is slack demand by market participants; the weakness of the housing market since the late 1980s is an additional factor. The infrastructure appears to be conducive to securitisation, and it should thus be rather easy to utilise techniques from the United States.

The United Kingdom has traditionally had adjustable-rate mortgages, and so building societies and banks have not had a strong incentive to securitise in order to reduce interest rate risk. Similarly, neither category of institution has had a severe problem with capital adequacy. On the other hand, since most MBS carry variable rates, they have not matched investor demand for fixed-rate assets. (In any event, many major categories of UK institution, such as pension funds and insurance companies, have tended to prefer equity investment.)

Despite the slow growth of the domestic market in securitised assets, London remains the most important European centre for securitisation. In many deals, receivables originated in other countries are structured as euro-market issues. (Related SPVs are often located in other centres such as the Channel Islands.) In addition, London plays an important role as a centre for the distribution of securitised products from the United States to European investors.

In 1993-1994, the volume of issues picked up somewhat. Many UK-based financial institutions believe that it is important to maintain some capacity to operate in the ABS markets in case demands should firm. Thus, a number of ABS issues have been made using an increasingly wide variety of collateral, such as automobile receivables, leases, nursing home loans, home equity loans and personal loans. In addition, in 1994 – for the first time in five years – a major bank issued an MBS and the first issue by a building society took place. In general, new issues have depended less upon third-party guarantees and more upon internal guarantees such as over collateralisation and spread accounts. Prospects for growth are seen as reasonably good, especially if final loan demand recovers.

In *France*, in the late 1980s, financial institutions and the authorities became convinced that securitisation could serve useful functions in the management of balance sheets. However, observing dissimilarities between French legal and regulatory systems and those which had proven suitable for securitisation in the United States and United Kingdom, the authorities were faced with the choice of relying on offshore issuance or seeking to develop distinctively French legal and regulatory structures for securitisation. In the event, the latter course was chosen.

In 1988, a law was enacted making it possible to transfer receivables into a *Fonds Commun de Créances* (FCC), which in many ways resembled a conventional SPV but which also bore some resemblance to a collective investment instrument. However, legal restrictions made it difficult to proceed with securitisation. These restrictions included a minimum two-year maturity on receivables, a requirement of homogeneity of assets in the FCC, and the prohibition on an FCC acquiring assets after its creation.

The prospects for securitisation brightened when revisions to the laws governing FCCs were enacted in 1992-1993. The amendments made it possible to securitise assets with less than two years maturity and to replenish assets inside a structured transaction. In addition, the 1988 law was amended to allow for simplification of procedures in cases of a change in the servicer. The French financial community generally believes that following the revisions of 1992-1993, the legislative framework is adequate to allow for an increased volume of securitisation.

Many French financial institutions are convinced that the prospects for expansion are excellent, and have set in place strong securitisation teams. Assets with particular potential for development are auto loans, leases and consumer loans. Through 1993, only one mortgage securitisation had taken place. This reflected the fact that many French mortgages were made at very low interest rates (often below the yield on government bonds), and would have entailed the recognition of losses by banks. Moreover, documentation on French mortgages is often not standardised.

Actual securitisation began in 1989 with an issue of broker/dealer loans (CAC-Titrisation). Through the end of 1994, a large number of deals with a total volume exceeding FF 66 billion have been launched, although many deals did not constitute "true securitisations", *i.e.* those involving a large number of homogeneous assets distributed to a broad investor base. A category sometimes characterised as "false securitisation" involved the creation of a bond-like instrument based on a single loan, often between affiliated financial institutions, which would be ineligible for issue as an ordinary bond. New issues were running at an annual rate of FF 17 billion francs in 1993-1994. In the latter year, a significant amount of MBS were launched for the first time.

All French securitisations have to date used the senior/subordinated structure for enhancement, with originators retaining subordinated tranches. This practice, which has not been accepted by the regulators of other countries, is under review by the French authorities.

In *Spain*, banks have been eager to explore securitisation as a funding mechanism, while the authorities have sought to assist the process in order to improve banks' funding capability and also to make it possible for the population to have wider access to housing finance. However, progress has been intermittent, as successive changes in the laws to support securitisation proved insufficient. An initial ABS issue backed by automobile receivables was made in 1990. In 1991, a law to allow for the issue of mortgage-backed securities was passed, but uncertainties surrounding the legal status of the vehicles to be created and prospects that the law would soon be revised tended to dampen investor interest. Two MBS issues were made in 1992, following which activity all but ceased.

During 1992, additional adjustments in legal mechanisms were made which further clarified regulations governing securitisation with the creation of special vehicles (*fondos de titulizacion*) compatible with Spanish domestic legal structures and special management companies (*gestoras*).

In the second half of 1993, MBS were issued for the first time. In January 1994, a Spanish bank announced the launch of a $1 billion asset-backed euro-commercial paper programme, supported by corporate loans. Despite continuing uncertainty about some legal provisions (*e.g.* possibilities for changes in servicers), most observers believe that the Spanish system is now robust enough to allow securitisation to proceed.

In *Italy* no MBS have been issued, but a small number of car loans and leases have been securitised mainly using offshore SPVs. The Italian banks are showing increased interest in using securitisation, and the authorities have also been studying the possibility of taking steps to enable banks to issue MBS and ABS. However, uncertainties with regard to several aspects of infrastructure, mainly the lack of a specific legislative and regulatory framework for securitisation impede progress. Other problems include taxation and legal aspects of the transfer of titles. Market participants hope that current efforts to adjust legal structures will maker wider securitisation feasible.

No securitisations have occurred to date in *Belgium*, but banks and the authorities see possible benefits in utilising these techniques. Since 1992, the parliament has been making major revisions to the relevant laws that should facilitate issuance of MBS and ABS. In addition, the banking authorities have indicated that they will accept off-balance-sheet treatment for assets that are sold, provided that all relevant risks are also transferred.

Some Nordic countries, notably *Sweden* and *Finland*, are in various ways examining the prerequisites for securitisation as a means of addressing some of the problems that have emerged in their financial systems. In particular, many of the major banks were decapitalised as a result of banking crises in the late 1980s and early 1990s, and some banks still hold comparatively large stocks of impaired assets. (Denmark did not experience a decline in bank credit standing that required a basic restructuring of its financial system.) In Sweden the authorities are examining the general legal conditions needed for securitisation. The official attitude is basically favourable to the growing use of securitisation as a constructive financial technique. New legislation will be implemented in order to lay the groundwork for domestic securitisation operations. In the meantime, a major Swedish bank operating through specialised subsidiaries has launched several issues backed by domestic mortgages. Since it was not deemed possible to initiate securitisation operations without changes in the domestic financial infrastructure, it was decided to launch the issues offshore, with the SPV located in Jersey. Through July 1994, nine issues totalling more than $1.3 billion equivalent had been floated.

The authorities of Finland decided to explore the possibility for securitisation to be widely used on a regular basis, following comprehensive rehabilitation of the banking system. In this connection, a major review of the domestic financial system (including relevant laws and regulatory practices) was undertaken to determine whether the domestic infrastructure would permit securitisation. A final report in 1993, concluded that it was appropriate to allow banks that are rehabilitated to utilise securitisation in re-shaping the financial system. (Of course, issues of bank rehabilitation, recapitalisation and privatisation would have to be resolved as well.) The report also concluded that no major infrastructure obstacles were present and recommended that any minor problems be removed. At the same time, the authorities made it clear that they were not actively promoting securitisation, but rather leaving open the possibility for banks to use this technique.

On the other hand, *Norway*, which also had a serious problem of banking insolvency, has decided not to use securitisation as a remedy.

In *Germany,* the strong financial position of most banks has obviated any immediate pressures to begin large-scale ''American style'' securitisation in order to bolster capital adequacy. In addition, the country has a well-developed system of mortgage finance, as described above, which has provided long-term housing financing at fixed rates while effectively solving the problem of asset/liability mismatches. Conceptually, the German universal banking law considers most securities business for customers to be banking; thus, there may be a strong presumption that banking disintermediation should not be encouraged. In addition, the banking supervisory authorities are unsympathetic to securitisation in the form of true asset sales, fearing that in case of liquidity and/or insolvency problems of the SPV, which itself primarily relies on an uninterrupted cash flow arising from the securities, there might be a moral or *de facto* obligation for the originating bank to buy back these securities in order to protect its own standing. At any rate, it is feared that the originating bank could not, in operations involving continuing asset sales, protect itself from a deterioration in the credit standing of the SPV; in that case, the continuing asset sale programme would have to be terminated or changed. Even the finance subsidiaries of German automobile companies are subject to universal banking law and thus would find it difficult to remove assets from balance sheets.

Nevertheless, a small amount of "American-style" securitisation has occurred. Some non-financial firms have launched ABS issues using offshore SPVs, and some German banks have created offshore asset-backed commercial paper programmes, partly funded with domestic assets. On the whole, however, Germany does not appear a most promising area of expansion for securitisation in the near future.

Similarly, in *Austria, Denmark, the Netherlands* and *Switzerland*, the combination of relatively strong domestic banks and well-developed alternative structures for mortgage finance have meant that demand for securitisation on the part of market participants is not especially strong. Additionally, the banking supervisors in Austria would have difficulties accepting off-balance-sheet treatment for bank assets. In Switzerland, the authorities have not yet taken a final decision in this regard.

In *Japan*, domestic securitisation has not progressed very far. Some factors would appear to make Japan a good candidate for securitisation. Securities markets have historically been important in intermediation and several Japanese securities houses are major players in all world markets – including ABS and MBS markets. Some in the securities industry believe Japanese securities houses, which now have serious problems with profitability, will need to become more active in the domestic fixed-income market. In addition, the decline in asset quality at Japanese banks has created a need to improve capital/asset ratios. At the same time, many banks are concerned by the possibility that securitisation might weaken close bank/industry relations, traditionally a distinguishing feature of the Japanese economy. Moreover, Japanese banks believe that reliance on securitisation might lead to a loss in basic corporate lending business, traditionally one of their principal sources of profit, and thus have not actively supported securitisation. Some initial consideration was also given to the use of securitisation to improve banks' capital/ assets ratios. For the time being however, a decision has been made to rely mainly on other means to deal with this problem.

The domestic legal status of ABS and MBS remains unclear. Even following some changes in the relevant laws in 1992, such instruments are not fully recognised as securities. It might still be possible to trade these instruments without designation as securities, albeit with lesser levels of investor protection and a narrower investor base.

In September 1994, the possibilities to engage in securitisation were broadened. The Ministry of Finance allowed leasing and consumer credit companies to sell receivables to offshore SPVs. Under the new rules, investment banks will be able to repackage the collateral for resale as ABS. The securities may be denominated in yen or in foreign currency. Initially, the ABS can be sold to foreigners or to certain categories of Japanese institutions, such as banks, trust companies or insurance companies. These securities will be eligible for resale to approved domestic investors after the customary 90-day waiting period, provided they are yen denominated. The issue of broader domestic use of securitisation is still under consideration.

Canada has programmes of government-sponsored mortgage-backed securitisation, partly patterned on that in the United States. In the mid-1980s the Canada Housing and Mortgage Corporation (CHMC) began a programme of insuring residential mortgages for fees. The CHMC assembles these into pass-through securities, which are the placed with investors. Some mortgages can be prepaid, and the resulting mortgage-backed securities will incorporate prepayment risk.

In 1988, a second programme was begun which in effect securitised multi-unit social housing (non-profit mortgages which are combined with programmes to provide subsidised low-income housing). In March 1993, the MBS market amounted to C$15 billion, compared with a total of C$ 280 billion in outstanding mortgages.

Despite a significant programme of government support for mortgages, close linkages to United States financial markets, and a financial infrastructure which would appear similar to that of the United States, the Canadian market in mortgage-backed and asset-backed securities remains proportionally much smaller than that of its southern neighbour. The relatively small size of the Canadian MBS market would appear to reflect: *i)* a tradition of adjustable-rate (as opposed to fixed-rate) mortgages; *ii)* a comparatively small number of nationwide banks; and *iii)* a banking system that has been better capitalised and that experienced relatively fewer strains than that of the United States in the 1980s. A somewhat less powerful and less independent securities industry than in the United States may also have been a factor slowing growth of the MBS market.

The market in asset-backed securities has grown more slowly than the market in mortgage-backed securities. Some asset-backed commercial paper programmes were begun in 1991, and estimates of the size of this market in early 1993 were on the order of C$ 3 billion. In 1991, bonds backed by automobile receivables were also introduced, followed by a series of deals backed by automobile leases. A small number of credit card securitisations have also taken place. Asset-backed issues other than the CP programmes are estimated at about C$ 3 billion at the end of 1993.

In *Australia* a moderate amount of structured financing has occurred, most of which has involved the securitisation of residential mortgages. A market in officially sponsored MBS exists, but unlike the United States and Canada – where the central governments have promoted the schemes – state governments have taken the lead. In 1984, the National Mortgage Market Corporation (NMMC), an entity partly owned by the State government of Victoria, issued promissory notes for the purpose of mortgage funding. In 1986, the first pass-through securities were issued by FANMAC, a similar organisation partly owned by the New South Wales Government. Currently, some twelve specialised mortgage companies are operating, two with participation by state governments. At the end of 1992, MBS outstandings amounted to A$ 6 billion, with FANMAC and NMMC accounting for nearly 70 per cent of this amount.

Asset-backed securities were first introduced in 1991. In June 1994, some A$ 2 billion were outstanding. The underlying collateral includes credit cards, public utilities' receivables, building leases, and local and semi-government debt. A few issues of asset-backed commercial paper have also been launched.

In *New Zealand*, the market is fairly narrow. A few MBS issues have taken place, but total issues amounted to only about NZ$ 1 billion. The ABS market is even smaller, with only one public issue floated: a NZ$ 150 million offering backed by credit card receivables. The relatively strong position of the banks, high start-up costs, and the small size of the domestic market have been the main factors inhibiting expansion.

Note and reference

1. For a discussion of the issues, see Boyd and Gertler ''Are Banks Dead? Or, are the Reports Greatly Exaggerated?'', *Federal Reserve Bank of Minneapolis, Working Paper 531, June 1994.*

Chapter 3

PROSPECTS FOR FURTHER INTERNATIONAL EXPANSION OF SECURITISATION

Securitisation is one in a series of innovations that have occurred in the capital market over the past two decades. Securitisation, which is now an important feature of the financial system of the United States, has been used on a small scale in a few other markets and in the euro-markets. However, it is still not certain whether the use of this technique will attain more significant proportions in the euro-markets and in the domestic markets of other OECD countries. As with most other innovations, market participants seek to apply the innovation in order to determine whether the new techniques are effective in dealing with concrete problems.

In examining the outlook for the worldwide growth of securitisation, it is possible to distinguish between two sets of pertinent factors. On the one hand, there are structural factors in the financial services industry which may favour further securitisation: the growing importance of institutional investors, the replacement of bank lending by capital markets in intermediation, the need to use bank capital efficiently, and the rising cost of funding for banks. Some countries have additional economic motivations to pursue securitisation, such as a reduction in bank capital owing to credit losses or an overhang of impaired assets.

On the other hand, as with many other innovations, the new technique may not be initially compatible with existing legal, institutional and regulatory arrangements in all countries. To the degree that questions of infrastructure impede securitisation, and there is a genuine desire to use the technique on a wide scale, the authorities must decide whether the existing infrastructure should be modified, and financial institutions must decide whether to ask the authorities to make such changes.

A. Structural trends in financial systems

While the United States still accounts for the overwhelming share of world securitised assets, financial institutions in many countries are actively seeking to develop this line of products in the belief that securitisation can represent an important addition to the techniques available to modern and efficient bank management. Securitisation can enhance the capability of bank management to control the overall asset and liability position of the institution. In general, securitisation can help banks to decide whether a given asset (with a given risk weighting) should be acquired, how the asset should be funded, whether capital should be raised to support a larger balance sheet or, alternatively, whether the asset should be removed from the balance sheet. Many banks have adopted decision models which assign risk-adjusted capital charges to each prospective operation, and these models serve as a guide to which assets should be held on the institution's balance sheet and which should be financed off-balance-sheet.[1]

The institutional pattern that has developed in most markets, including the major offshore markets, tends to favour alternative methods of financial intermediation (bank and capital market). Even when banks are major players in international securities markets, they tend to operate through separate capital market subsidiaries. Securitisation is a natural extension of this trend of two alternative channels for finance, and allows both the borrowing institution and the financial intermediary the greatest latitude in choosing the channel most appropriate for a given operation.

Off-balance-sheet securitisation fits in well with the observed shift from traditional lending to transactions-oriented banking in which the bank seeks to earn fee-based income rather than holding assets on the books for long periods and to hold as many assets as possible in tradeable forms. Increasingly, banks seek to have the flexibility of using on-balance-sheet or off-balance-sheet operations. Unlike the 1970s and early 1980s, when they still sought asset growth, banks in many countries are under internal pressures and constraints from supervisory authorities to maintain relatively high capital/ asset ratios. In the financial market of the future, banks may well earmark greater resources to payments services and the origination, ''packaging'' and servicing of investible assets, as opposed to traditional lending. Banks are therefore likely to seek a high volume of transactions but ultimately to retain a lesser share of assets than in the past. Thus, securitisation is a strategy that broadly coincides with the business plans of banks.

Although securitisation is a form of bank disintermediation, banks still participate in a number of ways. Banks can originate assets that are subsequently removed from their balance sheet. Alternatively, banks can devise structures under which assets never appear on their balance sheet and are sold directly to an SPV. In these cases, banks can create structures and participate as servicer or by offering liquidity or guarantee facilities. Examples of securitisation that completely bypasses the banking system are the mortgage companies in the United States, the SMLs in the United Kingdom, and asset-backed commercial paper programmes.

Some banks are now encouraging their corporate customers to sell receivables directly to domestic or offshore SPVs in order to issue ABS or asset-backed CP. Indeed, in countries where the volume of domestic securitisation is negligible, some institutions, are now regularly using funding based upon CP programmes in the United States or the euro-markets, a tactic which enables the bank to earn the fees from the CP programme without incurring a capital charge. Since the bank directs the borrower to a CP facility without ever holding the assets on its own balance-sheet, offshore CP issuance is also effective in cases where domestic regulations will not permit assets to be removed from balance sheets. The assets securitised in this manner are likely to be low-yielding claims on well-rated corporate borrowers.

The decline in the quality of bank balance sheets and the overhang of bank claims on distressed sectors – especially the real estate sector – mean that banks in several countries are intent upon reducing the size of their balance sheets and making as many assets as possible tradeable. With banks in a number of countries under pressure to maintain high capital/asset ratios, the impulse to reduce the size of the balance sheet should increase. Moreover, since many banks in many countries have been downgraded by rating agencies, the cost of funding through the interbank markets and of raising new capital has risen, thus making securitisation a relatively attractive option. Similarly, with lower ratings for banks, investors may prefer to hold securities which are backed by specific assets, rather than generalised claims against financial institutions.

In cases where a sizeable share of the banking system, or some other broad category of intermediaries, has become insolvent, securitisation can be part of a general programme to rehabilitate financial systems. As the experience of the RTC suggests, securitisation can be used both to sell good assets held by bad banks and to dispose of assets that are themselves impaired. In these cases, credit institutions may see asset sales as the best means of achieving adequate capital/asset ratios while preserving a role in intermediation.

The foregoing analysis would suggest that securitisation could be a useful tool in financial intermediation in many countries. However, as has been mentioned several times in this study, one of the great anomalies concerning securitisation in a global perspective is the extensive use of this technique in the United States and its rather limited application nearly everywhere else. If it is possible to cite a single point of divergence to explain why securitisation has been used so widely in the United States and so little everywhere else, the differing rates of growth of assets – and particularly of those in the late 1980s and early 1990s – is highly significant. Securitisation is one aspect of a distinctive pattern of intermediation that has characterised the financial system of the United States in the past few years. In particular, during the mid to late 1980s, United States banks began to slow the growth of total assets, and particularly of loans. In fact, loans of commercial banks showed virtually no increase at all in the early 1990s. That same period was one of exceptionally rapid growth of the MBS market, and it was during this time that the ABS market, including the market in asset-backed commercial paper, was launched. The period of slow bank asset growth was also a period of considerable financial activity. The volume of mortgage debt rose sharply, while the rate of mortgage refinancing was high in an environment of falling interest rates. At the same time, the savings and loan industry, a traditional source of on-balance-sheet mortgage finance, was in crisis and increasingly incapable of providing on-balance-sheet finance for residential mortgages. Part of the slack was taken up by direct mortgage lending from the commercial banks, but most of the gains were made in the form of MBS issues. (See Table 1 in the United States country note.)

The slowing of bank lending was part of a wider adjustment. The United States banks, having suffered major losses due to excessive, and often imprudent, loan growth and deteriorating credit quality through the mid-1980s, began to implement strategies based on tighter risk management systems and aggressive cost-cutting, while seeking higher capitalisation. In effect, the entire banking system was under intense pressure to use its capital more efficiently. (Indeed, considering the contraction that was occurring in the thrift industry, it may be said that depository institutions as a group were under enormous pressure to use their capital more efficiently than in the past.) In the adjustment, commercial banks tended to place emphasis on off-balance activities and non-interest sources of income. At the same time, tougher supervisory procedures, including requirements, were imposed. By the mid-1990s, following these adjustments, a marked strengthening of the financial position of United States banks had become evident.[2]

The slow rate of asset expansion by United States banks stands in stark contrast to the experience of other OECD countries, as can be seen in Table 2. In many of the countries experiencing rapid loan growth, banks encountered severe balance sheet problems in the late 1980s or early 1990s; in some, banks have remained relatively strong.

It should be added that in 1993-1994, with United States banks having largely completed their recovery, bank lending resumed at a moderate pace even as off-balance-sheet activity has continued. Nevertheless, it is clear that reliance on ABS and MBS

Table 2. **Growth of bank assets and credit in OECD countries, 1987-1992**

(change in per cent)

Country	Nominal terms		Real terms[a]	
	Assets	Loans	Assets	Loans
Australia	83	87	46	49
Austria	33	52	14	30
Belgium	33	58	14	35
Canada	40	37	19	16
Denmark	08	23	−7	6
Finland	104	106	65	66
France	62	61	41	40
Germany	68	75	45	51
Greece	125	63	−8	−37
Italy	67	18	22	59
Japan	40	63	29	51
Luxembourg	66	59	−1	−5
Netherlands	103	33	85	12
Norway	3	15	−12	−2
Portugal	34	100	25	07
Spain	70	82	22	31
Sweden	73	98	26	44
Switzerland	23	61	1	32
Turkey	1 235	1 115	9	0
United Kingdom	59	55	19	15
United States[1]	17	12	−4	−8
United States[2]	22	16	1	−4

1. Commercial banks.
2. Large commercial banks.
a) Nominal change/GDP deflator.
Source: OECD: *Bank Profitability, Financial Statements of Banks 1983-1992; Main Economic Indicators*, various issues.

issuance was one part of a larger process of de-emphasizing on-balance-sheet activity which characterised American banks during the period; it is equally clear that the banking systems of other countries did not adapt their behaviour as radically as that of the United States.

It is beyond the scope of this enquiry to analyse in depth the shift to off-balance-sheet activity by United States banks, or to predict whether the expansion of on-balance-sheet activities will now resume. Likewise, this study cannot give a definitive answer to the question of whether other countries are likely to follow the United States' example in shifting a larger share of operations to an off-balance-sheet basis.

There are other differences between the United States and other financial systems that may further explain why the application of securitisation has progressed so unevenly. Markets in consumer debt are often not as well-developed as in the United States. Documentation on such debt is generally not standardized and reliable historical data on payment are frequently not available in many countries. The depressed state of the real estate sector, usually one of the largest sources of securitised assets has compounded the initial difficulties in many cases. The institutional investor communities of most OECD countries lack the sophistication of that in the United States. Moreover, in many OECD countries, institutional investors are still subject to rather heavy regulation of portfolios, which makes it difficult to market innovative products such as MBS and ABS.

The preceding analysis should not be interpreted to mean that securitisation is not likely to take hold outside the United States. Indeed, in surveying the current situation of OECD countries, it is possible to identify a number of particular cases where financial institutions may be inclined to consider using MBS or ABS issuance as a means of strengthening capital/asset ratios while shifting a certain amount of business to an off-balance-sheet basis. Even the lack of strong domestic institutional investors need not be a fatal handicap. Domestically originated MBS and ABS can be marketed to international investors.

While the foregoing discussion applies mainly to OECD member countries, securitisation may have some applicability for non-Member countries as well. Many corporate or official entities from developing countries have been able to securitise receivables related to international trade or investment, and thus to achieve considerable savings in funding costs and/or to increase the total inward flow of financial resources. Similarly, securitisation may have some relevance to central and east European economies in transition in dealing with problems such as insolvent banking systems or in achieving privatisation.

B. Financial infrastructure

Experience has shown that, even assuming that market forces in the financial system are conducive to securitisation, an appropriate legal, regulatory, tax and accounting framework – *i.e.* an adequate financial infrastructure – must exist in order for domestic securitisation to proceed. Most of the mechanisms currently used in securitisation were developed in the United States, and thus reflected United States laws and practice. In attempting to transfer American techniques to other systems, incompatibilities may arise.

The basic mechanism for securitisation is for an "originator" to create a "Special Purpose Vehicle" (SPV) and to sell "receivables" to the SPV, which is designed solely for the purpose of holding and managing the receivables and for issuing securities. All payment flows in securitised operations are designated "receivables". The SPV is usually characterised as a "bankruptcy remote" entity, meaning that it has legal protection against claims arising from the bankruptcy of the originator. The notes, trust certificates or preferred stock issued by the SPV are designated "securities". The agreement between the SPV and the originator often provides for the originator to act as "servicer" or collection agent for the receivables; the servicer usually holds funds destined for the SPV for some time.

The legal status of SPVs is closely tied to the concept of "trusts" as it has evolved in Anglo-Saxon law. Through a trust, the ownership (*i.e.* legal title) in certain assets can be transferred to one or more trustees who are obligated under the terms of the trust agreement to employ the assets for the benefit of one or more beneficiaries. In many legal systems there are difficulties in creating such vehicles, which do not correspond to existing legal categories. It may be necessary to create them by reinterpreting or modifying existing laws. In the United States, laws initially designed to create trusts for inheritance proved to be adaptable for use as SPVs; in subsequent decisions, American law has specifically recognised the status of SPVs.

A basic question is whether the local legal system will allow for the transfer of title to the receivables. Even where laws allow for such transfers, some legal systems may require that debtors be given power to veto sale of claims or may at least require that debtors be formally notified. The assets that are easiest to securitise are those in which claims are held against large numbers of debtors (for example mortgages, consumer receivables, credit card receivables), in which case notification of all debtors may be impractical. There are related issues of debtor privacy and consumer protection. In cases where existing laws present such difficulties, there is a possibility for originators to modify future contracts to allow transfer, but such modifications would make it difficult to securitise existing claims.

Legal criteria in determining whether a "true sale" has occurred may differ among jurisdictions. Most legal systems make a distinction between a "sale" of assets and a "financing". Legal systems may not recognise the "bankruptcy remote" status of the SPV, or may not give investors sufficient protection in case of delinquency by the debtors. There are also uncertainties as to the protection accorded the investor in the event of servicer insolvency.

Even when legal systems are adapted specifically to assist in securitisation, problems in marketing the resulting product may ensue. Thus, in France laws were modified to allow the creation of Fonds Communs de Créances (FCC), which in many respects are similar to SPVs but which were designed to conform to French legal norms. However, the remaining differences are said by market participants to have caused some hesitation by lawyers, rating agencies and investors in other jurisdictions. That said, initial hesitancy may have been due to the relative lack of familiarity with FCCs; eventually, many French securitisations using the FCC structure have been rated AAA.

On the side of accounting and regulatory requirements, the most important question concerning the securitisation of bank-originated claims is whether a given operation qualifies for off-balance-sheet treatment. Additionally, the risk weighting assigned by banking regulators to various categories of securitised assets is a serious issue. In order for securitisation to be possible, the accounting and regulatory practices of the relevant jurisdiction should recognise the removal of the assets in question from the originator's balance sheet, *i.e.* that the transfer of assets to an SPV is a sale rather than a financing. The distinction between the two concepts depends upon the degree to which the originator relinquishes claims to the assets and to which purchasers of the assets have recourse to the originator. This distinction is similar to the legal issue of "true sale" mentioned above.

Accounting practices may differ in the degree to which residual liabilities for claims that have been sold are calculated. Similarly, the valuation of interests in collateral that has been removed from the balance sheet but which continues to produce earnings through a spread account must be estimated. Other serious accounting issues are to what degree positions of originators or servicers should appear on-balance-sheets, and how to account for interests in subordinated tranches. Securities regulatory bodies must decide whether they wish to allow the introduction of securitised assets for public listing or private placements. Changes in national securities laws are sometimes required.

Issues of taxation can be highly significant. Some jurisdictions may levy taxes on the transfer of assets and/or on cash flows (of payments by debtors into the SPV or of payment by the SPV to the investors). Taxes may be imposed on profits earned by investments inside the SPV (*e.g.* from investments of debtor receipts not yet paid to investors, which would be relatively significant in an arbitrage CMO). Taxes at any of these points may make securitisation uneconomical compared to other financing instruments. At the same time, the creation of vehicles which partly seek to minimise tax payments on certain kinds of operations within a structured finance operation may be viewed as forms of tax avoidance by tax authorities. Many jurisdictions impose taxes on payment of interest to residents and/or on bonds in domestic currency.

In cases where the domestic legal, tax or regulatory/accounting framework makes securitisation difficult, but where the law permits transfers of title, an alternative may be to structure a transaction in an "offshore centre" and to launch the issue in the euro-markets. This may involve changing the currency of denomination of the issue through a currency swap. For countries whose currency is not widely used internationally and which do not intend to function as major international financial centres, this may be an efficient means of gaining the benefits of securitisation without major changes in domestic infrastructure.

There may be some trade-off between creating a distinctive regime to conform to domestic legal and regulatory norms and developing a product that will appeal to international investors. If the securities are mainly intended for marketing to international investors, securitisation using an offshore SPV may be as efficient as creating a new domestic instrument that may be unfamiliar to international investors. Thus, Swedish financial institutions have securitised assets as euro-market deals, with the SPV established in the Channel Islands where tax laws are rather favourable. However, assuming that securitisation is to be used more widely in the Swedish financial system, specific domestic instruments will have to be developed, and some changes in the domestic infrastructure may be needed.

On the other hand, in France, the development of mechanisms compatible with domestic legal and regulatory structures was considered important from the beginning, since it was important to place securities with domestic investors. Furthermore, the French currency is increasingly used by international investors, and the competitive position of Paris as an international financial centre offering the full range of investment instruments is an important consideration for the authorities. Thus, more fundamental changes in the infrastructure were considered necessary to create specific French products that could be sold to both domestic and international investors. The experience of France suggests that the introduction of needed infrastructure requires considerable experimentation to remove all obstacles, and that the final product may not be immediately familiar to domestic and international investors.

A final issue of infrastructure is the adequacy of documentation and "back office" systems to support securitisation. The terms of loans and the documentation supporting loans that are used as collateral in securitised operations must be sufficiently standardized to permit the assembling of pools of homogeneous assets. For example, it has been observed that terms of commercial real estate loans are often negotiated in rather fine detail with each borrower, and that conditions (security, terms of repayment, etc.) vary to such an extent that the loans often lack the homogeneity need for inclusion in pools. In some countries, variations in loan documentation practices on residential mortgage or consumer loans may be such that investors have to study each proposed loan sale in detail, and it may not be possible to pool loans from different originators. Furthermore, it is important to be able to monitor payments, identify delinquencies and establish regular procedures to deal with delinquency if investors are to purchase assets with reliable cash flows. Credible histories of payments on specific categories of assets are also needed.

The high costs of perfecting the infrastructure needed for securitisation may seem particularly burdensome as a country begins the process of securitisation, because it is often not clear at the time whether certain necessary practices will be permitted under existing rules, or whether investors will find the resulting products attractive. Since the number of offerings that have been launched outside the United States is small, many countries are still in the phase when initial costs of finding suitable mechanisms are high in proportion to the volume of business. Similarly, investors may hesitate to purchase products with which they are not familiar and which may have uncertain liquidity. Presumably, as the number of offerings increases, standardised practices will evolve and liquidity will grow. Indeed, it is possible that in view of the efforts undertaken in the past few years, some countries may be close to finding workable mechanisms for securitisation.

Owing to the detailed work needed to perfect an infrastructure that allows securitisation to take place with products that will be accepted by investors, the process of elaborating an appropriate infrastructure is often time-consuming and expensive. The high start-up costs of securitisation may be particularly severe in Europe because of the large number of jurisdictions and the resulting problems in creating standardized products that can be distributed to a wide investor community. Unlike the United States, where securitised products tend to be standardized and saleable throughout the country, European securitisations have tended to reflect differences in several jurisdictions, and hence tend to be rather labour-intensive with considerable work by lawyers and accountants needed to initiate operations in each jurisdiction.

Notes and references

1. For an example of a decision model for securitisation versus retention on balance sheet, see Twinn, 1994. "Asset-backed Securitisation in the United Kingdom", in Bank of England *Quarterly Bulletin* 34 (May 1994).
2. For a discussion of this phenomenon, see Cantor and Demsets, 1993 – "Securitization, Loan Sales, and the Credit Slowdown", Federal Reserve Bank of New York *Quarterly Review,* (Summer 1993) Volume 18 No. 2.

achieved modest proportions. Countries in this category would include Australia, Canada, France, Spain, and the United Kingdom. In Japan, where domestic activity to date has been of minor significance, the authorities have taken a limited number of steps that enable market participants to engage in securitisation under carefully controlled circumstances. If activity were to accelerate, the authorities might consider further adaptations in the legal and regulatory framework in order to facilitate wider securitisation. In other countries (Belgium, Finland and Sweden), the authorities have modified their domestic systems or intend to do so to allow domestic securitisation to take place, but no domestic transactions have taken place to date. In the Netherlands and Denmark, the authorities have concluded that the domestic infrastructure would permit securitisation but no demand on the part of market participants has been noted. In Germany, the authorities have not taken any specific measures that would impede off-balance-sheet securitisation. Nevertheless, this technique is considered inherently riskier than other comparable techniques, and hence the authorities are likely to scrutinise all requests for off-balance-sheet treatment very carefully. Other Member countries, such as Austria and Norway, appear to be taking the view that current domestic legal and supervisory norms should not be modified to any considerable degree in order to accommodate securitisation. Switzerland has not yet made a decision in this regard. Finally, in Italy there are problems with infrastructure that might be serious enough to impede securitisation, while the underlying strength of demand by market participants is uncertain.

One pragmatic stance, which reflects the thinking that it would not be wise to take measures to thwart the expansion of securitisation but also that no measures should be enacted to provide positive support, is to allow differences between the domestic and the offshore markets to continue. In these cases, officials will permit securitisation to proceed through offshore markets, and thus allow domestic institutions to participate in the market, but will retain the specific character of their domestic infrastructure. This would leave domestic entities that are not subject to banking laws free to engage in securitisation by transferring assets to offshore centres. Such a policy is likely to be most effective if in the future securitisation continues to be a phenomenon that is confined to the United States and a few offshore markets, while remaining of minor importance in most domestic markets. If, however, securitisation becomes a major trend that characterises the markets of many OECD countries, more far-reaching changes in domestic financial structures will eventually become inevitable.

Although it may not be practical at this time to achieve a full consensus on whether domestic practices should be modified in order to accommodate securitisation, one area in which greater consensus would be desirable is the treatment of securitised assets by bank supervisors. The regulations regarding removal of assets from bank balance sheets and the risk weighting of securitised claims vary considerably among OECD countries. Some supervisors are concerned over the risk characteristics of securitised assets, both for the financial institutions originating them – which may retain some residual risk – and for the investors. Since much of the risk incurred in securitisation is off-balance-sheet and since structured financings are extremely complex, risks need to be carefully identified by supervisors and reflected in capital requirements.

One specific area in which considerable lack of uniformity in national policy can be detected is the weighting of MBS in the capital requirements applied to banks purchasing them. Table 3 shows the risk weighting assigned to MBS in OECD countries. A number of countries have taken the approach that MBS should be assigned the same weight as the underlying collateral. By this standard, an MBS should have a 50 per cent weighting, the same as applied to residential mortgages under BIS standards. (In the United States GNMA securities, which carry a full guarantee of a US Government agency, have a zero risk weighting while other MBS, including those supported by Federal agencies other than GNMA, carry a 50 per cent weighting.) Other countries, however, apply a 100 per cent risk weighting. It can be argued that assigning a higher risk weighting to one asset of equivalent risk than is assigned to an asset with similar risk (and usually with credit enhancement) constitutes a regulatory incentive to retain mortgages on-balance-sheet, rather than to securitise the assets.

Table 3. **Risk-weighting of mortgage-backed securities
in the portfolio of resident banks in OECD countries**

(percentage)

EC Members	
Austria	100
Belgium	100
Denmark	50
Finland	100
France	50
Germany	100
Greece	NA
Ireland	100
Italy	100
Luxembourg	100
Netherlands	100
Portugal	100
Spain	50
Sweden	50
United Kingdom	50
Other countries	
Australia	100
Canada	50
Iceland	–
Japan	100
Mexico	–
New Zealand	50
Norway	100
Switzerland	100
Turkey	–
United States	50[a]

a) Zero, for GNMA-backed bonds.
Source: OECD/DAF.

Divergences in regulatory practice are noticeable among EC member countries, even though the EC Directive on Solvency Ratios for Credit Institutions of 1989 was intended to harmonize relevant practices among EC countries. The Directive stated that with the exception of certain specified kinds of off-balance-sheet assets which were assigned lower weightings, all such claims would receive a 100 per cent weighting. Furthermore, the Directive assigns a 10 per cent weighting to mortgage bonds thorough 1998 and a 20 per cent weighting after that date. These guidelines would appear to give highly preferential treatment to mortgage bonds as opposed to MBS. Nevertheless, the practices of EC member states diverge significantly. Thus, some countries appear to be acting in accord with the principle that the Solvency Directive mandates a 100 per cent weighting for MBS, while others seem to conclude that the weighting should reflect the risk weighting of the underlying collateral.

The lack of consensus is somewhat disconcerting, since the trend in the past few years has been toward convergence of standards among bank supervisors. It may be unwise to allow large discrepancies in prudential rules to persist: they might lead to ''regulatory arbitrage'', where securitised assets would be booked in the jurisdiction in which treatment is most lenient.

Chapter 5

CONCLUSION: THE OUTLOOK FOR INTERNATIONAL SECURITISATION

As the discussion throughout this text has made clear, there is a continuing sharp divergence between the situation in the United States, where securitisation has already become an established feature of the financial system, and in the rest of the world, where activity is subdued and the outlook doubtful. While inadequacies in infrastructure may be an inhibition to securitisation in some countries, the major explanation for the limited use of these techniques is that demand on the part of market participants has been limited until now.

Probably the most significant point of divergence between the United States and other Member countries is that banks in the United States have shifted to off-balance-sheet activity to a far higher degree than have banks in other countries. The banks of most Member countries appear to have pursued balance sheet growth – particularly loan growth – as a business strategy, long after the banks in the United States discarded that strategy. Part of the difference may be that in a number of OECD countries bank capital has been adequate, and thus there has been no slowing of asset growth. However, loan growth was also rapid in countries which have experienced credit problems. It is uncertain whether in countries where scarcity of capital is a constraint on lending, created institutions will now seek to shift activity to an off-balance-sheet basis. Less well developed markets in consumer debt are another factor which slowed the advance of securitisation. Depressed real estate markets in some countries may have created additional problems, since residential mortgages are one of the more commonly used forms of collateral. Moreover, the process of developing the needed infrastructure and familiarising investors with new products tends to be prolonged, especially in Europe where there are a number of national prudential systems and investor communities.

Looking to the future, at least a moderate growth of securitisation appears likely. It is possible to identify some countries where prospects for growth appear reasonably good at this time. In those countries where a significant volume of ABS or MBS issuance has already occurred (*e.g.* France, Spain and the United Kingdom), activity in 1994 was reasonably brisk and should remain so in 1995 as well.

Beyond the markets where these practices are already established, prospects are also good in countries in which the appropriate infrastructure is (or will soon be) in place and where the need to use bank capital efficiently is strong due to problems of declining credit quality in the domestic banking system. Sweden and Finland would appear to be cases in point. These countries also might find securitisation a useful means of dealing with impaired assets.

In Japan, recent changes in regulations have made it easier to issue ABS and MBS. Once it becomes clear whether market participants have significant demand for these products, further modifications in infrastructure may be made.

In a few cases, MBS issuance could play an enlarged role in housing finance. The best prospects for expansion would appear to be in Finland, France, Spain and Sweden.

The cases listed above suggest that there are certain ''niches'' of the financial market where securitisation may grow. Whether a more generalised growth is likely is more questionable. As with other innovations that have appeared over the years, the ultimate test will come as market participants find whether securitisation is useful. Perhaps the greatest uncertainty in this regard is whether banks in OECD countries will shift to a pattern of slow asset growth with greater reliance on off-balance-sheet activity – whether the pattern which characterised the financial system of the United States from the mid-1980s until the early 1990s will ultimately become a feature of the world financial market of the future.

Chapter 6

COUNTRY NOTES

Australia

A moderately large amount of structured finance has occurred, with the securitisation of residential mortgages being most prominent. As at end June 1994, 73 per cent of the A$ 8 billion securitised market was mortgage-backed. The mortgage-backed security (MBS) market has been encouraged by official programmes to support housing, but unlike the United States and Canada where the central government has been active in promoting the market, the state governments took the lead in Australia. Due to constraints on state government borrowing in the 1980s, it became increasingly difficult for states to sustain public funding of low-cost housing; however, government support made it possible for low (and middle) income households to obtain finance for housing from certain intermediaries, effectively financed through a securitisation programme.

The securitisation market began in Australia in 1985 with the issue of promissory notes by the National Mortgage Market Corporation (NMMC), established in 1984 by the Victorian state government. In late 1986 the First Australian National Mortgage Acceptance Corporation (FANMAC) was formed by the government of the state of New South Wales. It was the first to issue investment grade, term securities. Each of these organisations has state governments as part owners, in conjunction with private sector shareholders. By June 1994, 27 organisations were involved in securitisation programmes (generally through trust structures), including about 15 in non-mortgage programmes. At this time, the two government-related issuers, FANMAC and NMMC, accounted for 32 and 34 per cent, respectively, of outstanding MBS. These issuers obtain pools of mortgages originated by financial institutions under government housing schemes. Originating institutions often retain no liability for defaults, and credit and liquidity support is provided by the governments involved.

The expansion of the MBS market was aided by important legal and regulatory changes. State stamp taxes were lifted and restraints that would have prevented state-based building societies and credit unions from selling assets were removed. The Australian Government's Housing Loan Insurance Corporation (HLIC) was permitted to insure pools of mortgages, rather than individual mortgages. Regulations covering certain categories of institutional investors were modified to permit investments in MBS. The establishment of rating agencies and the alignment of Australian ratings with those in other markets have made it easier to market securities with complex structures.

Securitisation has only had a marginal impact on the market for mortgage finance. Compared to A\$ 135 billion in residential mortgages outstanding through intermediaries at the end of June 1994, only A\$ 6 billion were in securitised form. The main institutions in the primary mortgage market are the commercial banks, which tend to keep mortgages on their balance sheets. Until recently, involvement by financial institutions as originators of MBS has been limited to a few building societies, credit unions and co-operative housing societies. Most mortgages in Australia are at variable rates, which can be changed periodically, at the discretion of the lending institution as market interest rates change, and have maturities of 20-30 years. However, in recent years a small market has developed in housing loans with rates capped or fixed for an initial period (sometimes up to 10 years). Typically, fixed-rate mortgage prepayment carries an interest penalty, generally of one month's interest for each year of the fixed-term remaining. The loans underlying the FANMAC and NMMC programs typically have carried interest rates fixed for long periods or indexed to the rate of inflation, and in the past have had no prepayment penalty.

Initially, FANMAC's issues were single-tranche pass-through securities, but more recently several issues have used a multi-tranche approach using collateralised mortgage obligation (CMO) techniques. Floating-rate coupon pass-through securities, straight mortgage bonds with bullet repayments, inflation-indexed bonds and short-term commercial paper instruments have also been used by various issuers. Most MBS issues have used a trust structure. Recently NMMC launched a substantial programme of variable rate bonds.

Since there is no direct central government programme to guarantee mortgages, credit risk can be a significant consideration (although, as noted above, some schemes have state government support). Credit enhancements have taken the form of insurance of individual mortgages, pool insurance, lines of credit, over-collateralisation, and senior/subordinated bond structures. In general, the credit rating of Australian MBS is high with around half-rated AAA, and all at least investment grade.

The spreads of MBS over benchmarks vary significantly. MBS trade at a spread over government bonds of similar maturity. Quoted yields on 3-year MBS at end June 1994 ranged from 65 to 90 or more basis points over Commonwealth Government Securities (CGS). The premiums in these spreads reflect credit risk, prepayment risk, and lesser liquidity. Market participants report that trading in MBS is rather subdued. (As a comparison, spreads on 3-year new South Wales Treasury Corporation bonds over CGS were around 20 basis points.)

There are no explicit legal obstacles to the further growth of the market. However, changes in 1992 to the Corporations Law have made access to the non-professional market difficult. Securitised programmes intended for the non-professional market have to comply with onerous reporting provisions under sections of the law which cover debentures and prescribed interests (*e.g.* trusts).

The guidelines of the Reserve Bank of Australia (RBA) have affected the prospects for the expansion of the MBS market. In order to allow the removal of assets from the books of a bank, the sale must be clean with no ongoing financial, commercial, or moral risk. Additionally, a 100 per cent risk weight is applied to all securitised assets held by banks. Thus, a residential mortgage would normally have a 50 per cent risk weight, but a security based upon a pool of mortgages (normally with credit enhancement) would carry a 100 per cent weight. (Note that from September 1994, a 100 per cent risk weight will be applied to housing loans having a loan-to-valuation ratio in excess of 80 per cent.) These guidelines encourage banks to hold mortgages on-balance-sheet rather than to securitise them. Similar rules have also been adopted by building society and credit union regulators. Recently, the Reserve Bank circulated to banks for comment revised prudential guidelines which permit more active involvement by banks in securitisation structures, subject to appropriate capital and disclosure requirements. The 100 per cent risk weight for all securitised assets is also under review.

The asset-backed securities (ABS) market (*i.e.* non-mortgage-backed issues) has shown marginal growth in recent years, with outstandings at end June 1994 estimated at just over A$ 2 billion (publicly and privately placed). Issues have been backed by credit card receivables, public utility receivables, building leases, and local and semi-government debt. Repackaging of bonds has also occurred. Some new issues of commercial paper have used a multi-purpose company structure (that is, the one vehicle is used for more than one securitised issue rather than the commonly used single-purpose vehicle).

Growth in securitisation has slowed in recent years. Reasons for the slow pace in securitisation include an increased focus by market participants on the risks involved in these investments (following increasing prepayment on high fixed-rate mortgages such as those underlying FANMAC bonds – in a falling interest rate environment); the inclusion of securitisation under government borrowing limits (unless the sale of receivables is without recourse), limiting the attractiveness of securitising state government utilities' receivables; reporting requirements under the Australian Corporations Law; and mortgage pool insurers becoming more particular.

At this time prospects for expanded MBS issuance are mixed. From the side of the banks, incentives to securitise are small. The practice of granting variable-rate mortgages has prevented the emergence of large funding mismatches while the nationwide presence of major banks has reduced geographic concentrations. The high spread between mortgage rates and other interest rates has meant that mortgages have very attractive rates of return while the high cost of creating MBS (credit enhancements, liquidity facilities, etc.) would mean an erosion of the current high profitability of this business. Recent problems with the housing scheme underlying FANMAC bonds (which have had the effect of accelerating prepayments) has also slowed growth of the market. On the other hand, given the returns on these assets, the investor community in time may be willing to absorb an increased volume of offerings. Securitisation activities may be boosted by the proposed amendments to the Reserve Bank's prudential guidelines, mentioned above.

Austria

Although off-balance-sheet securitisation is relatively insignificant in Austria, the country has a rather well developed system of mortgage bonds. The universal banking system, which in many respects resembles the system in Germany, prevails in Austria with banks predominating in virtually every sphere of the financial system. The domestic capital market is of relatively small significance, even in comparison to other countries with universal banking. Nevertheless, Austrian schilling-denominated bonds have attracted some international investor interest and this may be a spur to development of the capital market.

There are several categories of financial institution, but in keeping with the principle of universal banking most institutions can engage in a broad range of activities. In the field of housing finance, the building societies *(Bausparkassen)* engage in partly subsidised housing lending under special savings-promotion programmes. The system of mortgage bonds *(Pfandbriefe)* dates back to the nineteenth century. Only a limited number of institutions are authorised to issue *Pfandbriefe*, specifically: *a)* there are two large banks, *Creditanstalt-Bankverein* and *GiroCredit AG*, which resulted from incorporation of mortgage banks into larger banking organisations; *b)* the nine state mortgage banks *(Landes-Hypothekenbanken)* one of which is found in each state *(Land)* but which lend nationwide, and *c)* a central mortgage institution *(Pfandbriefstelle* der Oesterreichischen Hypothekenbanken) on some occasions has granted refinancing credit to the state mortgage banks and issued mortgage bonds in its own name. In addition, securities supported by receivables from local authorities (communal bonds) are found. Together, these institutions, which are called the *Pfandbriefe institutions,* accounted for the preponderant share of total housing finance and banks loans to public authorities.

Mortgages are generally for rather long terms, with 15-30 years common. Interest rates tend to be fixed, but banks can revise rates after specific periods of time have elapsed to reflect changed market conditions. Borrowers have the right to prepay mortgages at any time.

Pfandbriefe are used to manage interest rate risk by banks, while offering security to investors. The issue of these instruments is closely linked to the granting of long-term credits by credit institutions. The bonds have maturities of up to 15 years. The *Pfandbriefe* contain a call option allowing the issuer to redeem the bonds after a specified period. This option is exercised by the issuers when market interest rates diverge significantly from the rates on underlying mortgages. Banks can issue secured bonds (so-called funded bank bonds), which fulfil a similar role in funding.

The *Pfandbriefe* and communal bonds together accounted for only 20 per cent of total bonds outstanding at the end of 1992, considerably less than in most other countries with well-developed markets in mortgage bonds. Other bank-issued bonds account for approximately 30 per cent. Almost all other bonds are debts of the Austrian public sector, especially the central government.

Pfandbriefe provide high levels of security to investors. The law lays down stringent provisions concerning the level and nature of mortgages used in *originating* assets that bear the name *Pfandbriefe*; other secured bonds may be issued using other collateral. According to the law, holders of *Pfandbriefe* are senior creditors who are to be paid before all other investors in a failed institution. The law lays down fairly stringent requirements with regard to mortgages that can be used to support *Pfandbriefe*. *Pfandbriefe* use mortgages on residential, commercial or agricultural real estate as collateral.

Pfandbriefe are issued on tap by the originating institution which also has an obligation to repurchase these assets at prices based on market prices for government bonds. *Pfandbriefe* are listed on the Vienna Stock Exchange. A prospectus is required upon issue.

The main investors in *Pfandbriefe* are individual investors, insurance companies and collective investment funds; banks are only small net investors in these assets. The *Pfandbriefe* are one of the assets that can be used by insurance companies in meeting contractual payments used on insurance policies. Other assets are bonds issued by the central government or local governments. Given the relatively narrow range of domestic paper for investment, domestic demand for *Pfandbriefe* remains adequate to absorb new issues at competitive rates. International investor interest is small.

In general, the Austrian banking system has shown little interest in off-balance-sheet securitisation of assets, since the major Austrian banks are adequately capitalised. Moreover, the local investor community is not very strong. In Austria off-balance-sheet securitisation of assets is not in accordance with the accounting standards for banks.

Belgium

In Belgium, the securitisation market is yet to be created. Notwithstanding their high ratings and solid capital adequacy ratios, the country's major credit institutions have started to show interest in securitisation as a way of managing their balance sheets and financial risk.

Apart from the need for a suitable legal framework, the development of securitisation in Belgium poses the problem of constituting homogeneous debt portfolios and appropriate structures to manage and supervise them. A number of major credit institutions are exploring the possibility of securitisation.

It would therefore be useful to take a closer look at the Belgian mortgage market:

As of 31 December 1993, Belgian credit institutions held some BF 1 362 billion in outstanding mortgages, representing 21 per cent of their total loans. Most of these mortgages are residential.

Traditionally, credit institutions have financed mortgage lending by tapping their base of low-cost (regulated) passbook savings accounts and by issuing a steady stream of fixed-rate notes with maturities of between one and five years. The average residential mortgage spans 20-25 years and covers 70 per cent of the value of the underlying property.

New legislation on mortgage lending (the Act of 4 August 1992) allowed interest rates to vary periodically, effective 1 January 1993. But it also imposed certain conditions: variable rates had to be linked to benchmark indices based on yields on Belgian Government securities, and contracts had to specify the maximum amount (which could be set freely) by which the rate of interest could differ from the initial rate. Moreover, it left borrowers the option of choosing between a fixed rate and a variable one.

Considering the cost to credit institutions of administering and securitising mortgages, and the risk premium due to investors, it is generally acknowledged that a premium of nearly 200 basis points over the yield on Belgian public debt is needed for mortgage securitisation to be profitable.

At year-end 1993, the base mortgage rate (for new customers) was about 9.4 per cent, compared to some 6.6 per cent for government bonds. While the spread seems theoretically attractive, and the downward trend in Belgian long-term interest rates in 1993 would appear conducive to mortgage securitisation, the yield curve will still have to return to normal before the return on such securities will be sufficiently advantageous.

Adding to that is the fact that a substantial proportion of mortgages carry preferential rates, which were granted with a view towards building long-lasting relationships with individual clients. The lower margins on such loans therefore make it rather doubtful that they could be securitised.

To date, two proposed securitisation transactions have been submitted to the supervisory authorities: one – concerning capital leases – by a mid-sized credit institution, and another – regarding a portfolio of corporate loans – by a large institution. Neither was finalised.

At the time of its review of the aforementioned securitisation transactions, the Banking and Finance Commission (*Commission bancaire et financière* – the prudential supervisory authority for credit establishments) adopted the principle that, from the standpoint of prudential supervision (and particularly as regards the application of the regulations governing equity), the transfer of a debt portfolio could not be deemed fully-fledged (with the claims comprising that portfolio removed from the transferring credit establishment's balance sheet) unless the risks attaching to those claims were transferred completely and definitively.

Legal aspects

As part of the overall process of modernising the country's financial markets, the Belgian parliament recently adopted a number of measures to create a legal framework for the securitisation of debt.

First, the Act of 5 August 1992, amending that of 4 December 1990 on financial transactions and financial markets, made securitisation subject to the same rules as those governing collective investment undertakings (CIUs). In effect, it created a new type of CIU – an undertaking for investment in debt (UID) – which was to serve as a financial vehicle for the off-balanc-sheet securitisation of debt.

The fact that this securitisation vehicle has been set into the legislative framework applicable to collective investment undertakings implies that the new financial vehicle is, to a large extent, subject to the rules that govern other CIUs (and, in particular, to rules relating to supervision by the Banking and Finance Commission, the issuing and marketing of shares, and restrictions and taxation).

The Royal Order of 29 November 1993, implementing the aforementioned Act, sets forth the specific rules applicable to the new financial vehicle and to other parties to a securitisation transaction.

The new financial vehicle has the following features:
- Its sole purpose is collective investment in debt.
- Two legal forms are possible: contractual joint ownership (funds for investment in debt), or incorporation (companies for investment in debt).
- It draws its funds, at least partially, from the general public; but, in order to protect investors, the public may be solicited in respect of non-subordinated debt issues only.

- It should nonetheless be noted that rules are currently being drawn up for a new category of UIDs reserved for institutional investors.
- Above a fixed amount of statutory share capital, which may be no less than BF 1 250 000, total capital is variable.
- It has a set number of shares, which may not be redeemed by the holders from the undertaking's assets.
- It is not authorised to reinvest net returns on assets.

In the mechanism set up by the Act of 5 August 1992 and its implementing order, roles were conferred on a number of parties in addition to the new investment undertakings themselves:

- Each undertaking for investment in debt must be run by a management company, which handles general administration and accounting along with managing the vehicle's investments.
- This management company may, depending upon the terms of the debt collection agreement, assign responsibility for collection to the transferor or to a third party.
- The investment undertaking must have a depositary, responsible for keeping the UID's assets and doing with them as instructed by the management company; it must also monitor whether the performance of the debt portfolio and of financial flows differs markedly from the projections of the financial plan, and whether specific events might be likely significantly to alter the portfolio's risk profile or forecast outturns.
- Lastly, the management company is required to have contracted with a rating agency for the assessment of the securities issued by the UID.

The parties above are subject to specific regulatory obligations and restrictions, and notably to those regarding conflicts of interest.

Publicly issued shares in the vehicle are required to be listed on the stock market.

In addition, other regulations govern supervision, accounting, earnings allocation, redemption, alterations, provisions and fees, asset mix, and liquidation.

The Royal Order of 29 November 1993 stipulates the conditions under which foreign undertakings for investment in debt may operate in Belgium. As a rule, only those UIDs that are subject, in their country of origin, to supervision equivalent to that exercised over Belgian UIDs by the Banking and Finance Commission may start up operations in Belgium. In addition, they must also be subject to the same sort of rules as Belgian undertakings.

Organising securitisation in Belgium next required major reform of the procedures for the transfer of debt and its effect *vis-à-vis* third parties. The formal procedures for giving transfers such effect – *i.e.* notification of the debtor or the latter's acceptance of the transfer by notarial act (Article 1690 of the Civil Code), as well as annotation of the mortgage register, for preferred debt and mortgages (Article 5 of the Mortgage Act) – were considered very cumbersome and costly, and hence as obstacles to securitisation.

To rectify this, parliament adopted a number of measures that substantially modified the conditions for the transfer of debt and its effect *vis-à-vis* third parties. The changes applied to ordinary law as well as to the specific areas of mortgage lending and consumer credit.

The Act of 6 July 1994, amending the Act of 17 June 1991 organising the public credit sector and public sector holdings in certain private financial companies, as well as the Act of 22 March 1993 on the regulation and supervision of credit establishments, radically altered the ordinary law applicable to the transfer of debt and its effect *vis-à-vis* third parties.

Henceforth, the conclusion of a transfer contract is sufficient to give the transfer of debt effect *vis-à-vis* third parties, other than the debtor. The transfer has effect *vis-à-vis* the debtor only after the latter has accepted the transfer or been notified thereof. The requirement that transfers must be notified or accepted by notarial act, which had effectively prevented securitisation from getting under way in Belgium, was thus abolished.

In the event that a transfer of mortgages or of secured preferred debt takes place in connection with a securitisation transaction, Article 51 of the Act of 4 August 1992 on mortgage credit, as amended by the aforementioned Act of 6 July 1994, derogates from the special provisions that govern such a transfer's effect vis-à-vis third parties. Accordingly, the transfer of a preferred debt or of a mortgage by or to an undertaking for investment in debt, or the pledging of such a debt by or on behalf of such an undertaking, shall have effect on third parties without the transfer's having to be recorded as an annotation to the initial mortgage register. Notwithstanding, the person transferring or pledging the debt is required, should a third party so request, to furnish the necessary information regarding the identity of the transferee or the pledgee.

Pursuant to Article 25 of the Act of 12 June 1991 on consumer credit, a consumer loan agreement or a debt arising therefrom may be transferred only to those persons designated by law or authorised under the terms of the law, or to other persons designated by the King. The collective investment undertakings referred to in Book III of the Act of 4 December 1990 on financial transactions and financial markets, among which financial vehicles intended to be used in connection with securitisation (see above) are now included, are explicitly listed as persons authorised by law.

In the interests of consumer protection, Article 26 of the same Act derogates from ordinary law by stipulating that the transfer of a consumer loan agreement or of a debt arising therefrom shall theoretically not have effect *vis-à-vis* the debtor until the latter shall have been informed of the transfer by registered letter, except if such transfer is explicitly provided for in the loan agreement and if the transferee's identity is mentioned in the loan offer. Notwithstanding, the aforementioned Act of 6 July 1994 renders this provision inapplicable if the debt is transferred by or to an undertaking for investment in debt.

As a result, the law now enables and facilitates the securitisation of debt arising from consumer loan agreements.

Canada

Canada has a significant MBS market, although even allowing for differences of scale, it does not approach the proportions of the US market. Before the increased volatility in interest rates of the early 1970s and the resulting risk of maturity mismatches, Canadian mortgages tended to be for long terms and at fixed rates. Subsequently, adjustable-rate mortgages became the norm. At this time, mortgage rates are usually fixed for one, three or five years, after which the rate is reset. Amortisation takes place continually and the term for the entire mortgage may extend up to thirty years. Some Canadian mortgages contain prepayment options while others do not. Generally, the penalties for prepayment are less at the time in which interest rates are reset than at other times.

In the the early 1980s, very high short-term rates posed a risk of mismatch that banks were hesitant to accept. Consequently, market participants urged the authorities to consider the possibility of developing an officially supported MBS market, such as existed in the United States. In addition to lessening mismatches, it was argued that the creation of such a market would benefit consumers through longer-term mortgages and lower rates.

After an examination of the experience in the United States and other relevant data, it was decided to develop a Federally sponsored MBS programme supported by official guarantees. Under the system that was put in place by the National Housing Act, the Canada Mortgage and Housing Corporation (CHMC), a federal agency, guarantees payment principal on insured mortgages and also provides support for payment of interest, in return for fees. Homogeneous single family prepayable residential mortgages are pooled and sold to investors. These securities are described as "modified pass-throughs" in that only part of the interest is passed through to investors with a portion also retained by the originator as profit.

The development of the MBS market enabled smaller institutions such as regional trusts and mortgage bankers to access the capital markets directly, thus leading to greater competition in the mortgage market and – according to some analysts – to lower interest rates to borrowers. Although the possibility exists for lenders to offer longer-term fixed-rate mortgages while minimising interest-rate risk, variable rate instruments still account for nearly all mortgages.

With the original programme successfully launched, in 1988 the coverage was broadened to include securities backed by mortgages on multi-unit social housing, which was subsidised by the government. Since these mortgages do not have prepayment options, the Canadian MBS market now has both kinds of product.

Initially, individual investors were the main purchasers in the MBS market, but institutions now predominate. Nevertheless, these assets still are popular with retail investors, especially for inclusion in tax-advantaged retirement plans. MBS which are rated AAA and carry government guarantees traded at spreads of 65-90 basis points above comparable government bonds in 1992 and early 1993, but the spread fell to some 40-60 basis points by the end of 1993.

The MBS market has grown steadily since its inception. By the end of 1993, outstanding volume was on the order of C$ 16 billion, compared to total domestic residential mortgages of C$ 280 billion. The MBS market remains concentrated in officially guaranteed paper. Some attempts have been made to launch private label CMOs, but thus far only modest investor interest has been evinced. Due to the relatively short effective interest-rate maturities of Canadian mortgages, the trend to variable rates, and the lesser importance of prepayment risk, the Canadian market has not developed the complex multiple tranche collateralised mortgage obligations such as are found in the United States.

Most banks and securities houses have developed some capability to deal in the market, while investors are now accustomed to holding some MBS in their portfolios. In general, the major Canadian banks are not aggressively promoting the MBS market; most banks are reasonably well-capitalised and the issue of MBS is used as are other funding techniques such as interbank borrowings, Eurobond issues or swaps. However, other institutions such as mortgage companies, trust companies or credit unions can obtain funding more advantageously through MBS issuance than through alternative sources. Nevertheless, banks originated more than 50 per cent of all MBS pools in 1993. Overall, the potential for growth of the market seems reasonably solid, if not spectacular. The Canadian authorities are willing to grant off-balance-sheet treatment to assets securitised through the CHMC programmes and MBS carry a 0 risk-weighted capital charge. Consequently, banks may eventually wish to use this technique to remove assets from their balance sheet while retaining some earnings from the asset. Meanwhile MBS offer banks a product that carries little risk and can add to returns on assets. Investors also have some demand for assets of this kind which offer low-risk with higher yields than government paper.

The asset-backed securities market has shown moderate growth. With the development of the MBS market, many market participants believed that the ABS market would soon begin to expand. However, a number of legal and accounting uncertainties inhibited the emergence of a thriving ABS market until 1989 when the first issues appeared. The earliest and still the largest single sector in the ABS market is in asset-backed commercial paper. Since Canada has a deep well-functioning commercial paper market, there was great familiarity with the product on the part of both issuers and investors. Most of the issues to date have been bank-advised multi-vendor facilities with enhancements provided by bank letters of credit. The major banks have used this technique as a means of continuing fee-based relations with major corporate customers while conserving capital. Overall, outstandings under Canadian asset-backed commercial paper programmes were estimated at about C$ 3 billion at the end of 1993.

Following the introduction of asset-backed commercial paper, major corporations have shown increased interest in term asset-backed financings. Thus far, automobile-related receivables have been the most widely used form of collateral in the ABS market, with department store receivables also commonly used. In an initial operation in 1991, automobile receivables for Chrysler (Canada) with maturities of 6-42 months were used as collateral to support bullet bonds with semi-annual coupons of varying maturities which corresponded to the expected cash flows on the collateral. Enhancement took the form of senior/subordinated structure. The bonds were privately placed. Investor reception was good and subsequent issues carried progressively tighter spreads over government paper. Following several similar automobile-related issues by Chrysler, a series of issues were launched, supported by automobile receivables from other companies and credit card receivables. ABS issues, excluding asset-backed commercial paper, are estimated to be about C$ 3 billion.

In general, the prospects for further expansion of the ABS market appear reasonably promising. The market reception for most issues to date has been rather good and both banks and corporates are examining the possibility of increasing the volume of ABS issues based upon receivables such as automobiles and credit cards as well as personal loans, commercial mortgages and equipment leases.

Denmark

The Danish system of mortgage finance was begun some two hundred years ago. Since the 19th century the specialised mortgage credit institutions (MCIs) have been the major providers of mortgage credit. The system of financing housing through the issuance of mortgage bonds has resulted in a mortgage system which places greater reliance on the capital market than in any other European country.

The mortgage system has undergone major changes in the last quarter of a century. Traditionally, the system has been heavily regulated. During the 1980s and the beginning of the 1990s, however, the mortgage market has been gradually deregulated, so that the existing system can be characterised as generally market-based. At this time, the only constraints on the activities of the MCIs are prudential regulations and the legal regime which limits the functions of MCIs to mortgage finance.

In the 1970s and 1980s restrictions were imposed on the establishment of new MCIs. The number of MCIs was in this period only five; three of the institutions were generalised institutions, and two smaller institutions were specialised in industrial and agricultural lending, respectively.

Since restrictions on the establishment of new MCIs were removed in 1990, newly established MCIs must be organised as private, limited companies while existing institutions were given the options of remaining mutual associations or transforming themselves or into stockholder-owned companies. All Danish MCIs are now indeed organised as limited liability companies.

One distinctive feature of the Danish system is that before the 1990 deregulation, the MCIs functioned completely separately from the banking system. (In most other countries with well-developed mortgage bond systems, specialised mortgage institutions are usually subsidiaries of banks.)

Since 1990, a number of new MCIs have been formed, mainly by banks. These new MCIs are organised as independent companies, but unlike the traditional MCIs they function as a part of bank-led financial groups. Their funding methods and activities are the same as the traditional MCIs.

Except for the one MCI specialised in agricultural lending, the MCIs are included in the definition of credit institutions under EC directives and therefore must fulfil the EC capital adequacy requirements. All MCIs engage in on-balance-sheet finance of residential property and associated activity. MCIs also have the possibility other kinds of bonds (*i.e.* other than mortgage bonds) in connection with mortgage finance. In fact, the issue of non-mortgage bonds has been used in funding operations outside Denmark. The Danish MCIs do not take deposits, but fund themselves by issuing mortgage bonds (*realkreditobligationer*) which are listed on the Copenhagen Stock Exchange. Currently, the most common kind of bond is the annuity bond with principal and interest being paid throughout the life of the loan. There are also some serial bonds featuring constant principal payments but declining periodic total payments. There exist a limited number of bullet bonds with all principal repaid at maturity. Most of the mortgage bonds are callable, meaning that the borrower has the option to prepay. The prepayment risk is a major explanation of the spread between mortgage bonds and government bonds.

Most mortgages and mortgage bonds are at fixed rates. Residential mortgage bonds are typically issued with an original maturity of 20 or 30 years. The maturity of bonds issued for the funding of industrial projects would typically be shorter.

Mortgage bonds are considered to have a low credit risk. The main reasons for this are the limits on borrowing on property (loan-to-value) ratios and the regulations on market risks, which set limits on interest rate risk, foreign exchange risk and the mismatches between payments on the borrowing and the lending side for the MCIs. Furthermore, investors in mortgage bonds would be the most senior creditors in case an MCI were to be liquidated. The traditional ''joint and several'' guarantee of borrowers (see below) has further tended to diminish credit risk.

The main investors in mortgage bonds are domestic institutional investors (pension funds and insurance companies) which have a natural demand for longer-dated securities to match their liabilities. Foreign investors at the end of 1993 held less than 5 per cent of the total outstanding mortgage bonds.

Mortgage credit institutions grant fixed-rate mortgages, usually with quarterly repayments. In residential financing, borrowing may not exceed 80 per cent of the assessed value of the property and the maximum maturity is set at 30 years. Commercial banks will sometimes grant credits for that part of the purchase price which exceeds 80 per cent.

When obtaining a mortgage on property through one of the MCIs, the borrower receives the proceeds from sales of bonds. The borrower pays a margin – around $1/2$ to 1 per cent – above the interest payments due on the mortgage bonds. In the past, borrowers traditionally had joint and several responsibility, within limits, for the payments of principal and interest on loans in a pool. The joint and several responsibility of borrowers was counted as an element in the total capital of MCIs. The EC Directive on solvency ratios for credit institutions called for the Danish system of joint and several responsibility to be phased out by the year 2000.

Despite the country's small size, the Danish fixed-income market is one of the biggest in Europe. There was in mid-1993 around DKr 800 billion (around $125 billion) in mortgage bonds outstanding, which accounted for 60 per cent of the Danish bond market. In recent years there have been major efforts to improve liquidity in the mortgage market and to develop new products, which better match investor preferences.

The Danish mortgage market has experienced some significant strains in the past few years with a general decline in the financial strength of MCIs. Meanwhile, with new MCIs becoming increasingly important in mortgage finance, competition has intensified.

Since 1986, housing demand and prices have fallen significantly. Prepayment rates have increased substantially since 1988/89. Moreover, after-tax profitability for MCIs declined after the removal of favourable tax status in 1987. There was a record level of mortgage defaults in the last few years. Despite these difficulties, all bondholders have received full and prompt payments and the joint and several responsibility of mortgagees has never been invoked.

The mortgage bond market has many of the characteristics of mortgage-backed bonds both in terms of low risk to investors and the possibility for MCIs to pass market risks on to investors. Thus there has been no great pressure to develop off-balance-sheet mortgage finance. However, with the domestic mortgage market evolving rapidly, some institutions may in the future wish to utilise techniques of off-balance-sheet finance, such as it exists in major international markets. Although no "off-balance-sheet" securitised transaction has yet been attempted in Denmark, there are no apparent legal or regulatory impediments.

There have been no asset-backed securitisations in Denmark. At the same time, although the capital position of the Danish banks and other financial institutions has been adequate hitherto, interest in asset-backed securitisation could develop.

Finland

The Finnish financial system has traditionally been dominated by banks. Bond markets have played only a peripheral role, and mortgage bonds are not a particularly important financial instrument. However, with the weakening of the banking system since 1990, the authorities and the banks are considering the use of securitisation, both as a funding technique and as a means of dealing with impaired assets.

Finland has traditionally had a financial system in which banks are pre-eminent. Bank deposits (which have been favoured in the tax system) have been the principal means of holding assets, with bond, equity and money markets far less important. In the past the system was highly regulated, but in the 1980s considerable easing of controls took place. Although the bond and equity markets gained somewhat in importance, the main structural change in the financial system during the 1980s was that banks depended less upon deposits and more upon money market borrowing; bank deposits declined from 74 per cent of all financial assets in 1980 to 43 per cent in 1992, with money market assets rising from 1 per cent to 22 per cent. During the same period, bonds rose from 17 per cent of all assets to 25 per cent. Throughout the decade, banks remained the predominant players in the financial system by a wide margin.

The mortgage banks are subsidiaries of commercial banks. Most were established early in the twentieth century, but they have never been important in the financial system. In 1992, the mortgage banks accounted for only 2.6 per cent of total lending. Mortgage banks may issue both secured or unsecured bonds; their lending has mainly been to the business and local government sectors, rather than for housing. Housing finance has been provided directly from commercial banks which have not traditionally used bonds to fund their mortgage portfolios. The National Housing Fund, which is active in the market, also issues mortgage bonds. Mortgages on commercial industrial agricultural or residential property can serve as collateral for mortgage bonds. It is the practice to have a maximum loan-to-value ratio of 60 per cent. Total mortgage bonds outstanding at the end of 1992 amounted to Mk 27 billion (Mk 20.2 billion issued by mortgage banks and Mk 6.8 billion by the National Housing Fund) of a total bond market of Mk 162 billion.

The main impetus to consider securitisation has come from the decline of balance sheet quality in the banking sector since 1990, which required large-scale government intervention. In September 1991, the Bank of Finland took control of Skopbank (a commercial bank that also serves as the central bank for the savings banks), while removing impaired real estate commercial and equity loans from the balance sheet of

Skopbank and placing them in a special holding company. Over the next two years as the crisis persisted, additional injections of capital into several institutions as well as special guarantee funds were required. In effect, control over most banks has been acquired by the government.

As a result of the virtual collapse of the banking system, the authorities face two serious problems: *a)* to create a new financial system with newly-capitalised institutions, and *b)* to deal with the large stock of impaired assets. The authorities are examining the possibility of using securitisation for both purposes. In September 1992, the Ministry of the Environment established a Working Group, composed of officials and representatives of private banks, to consider the feasibility of using securitisation for housing loans under Finnish law and regulatory practices.

In May 1993, the Group ended its work and concluded that in general there were no major obstacles of a legal, fiscal or regulatory nature to the wide use of securitisation. Among the major specific conclusions were:

i) Finnish law allows for the transfer of claims among creditors. The Financial Supervision Authorities will announce the specific criteria that must be fulfilled if an originator is to achieve off-balance-sheet treatment (true sale) for its securitised assets. During 1994 the Financial Supervision will also issue other general guidelines for securitisation. The group recommended certain safeguards to assure that a debtor's liability is not increased as a result of the transfer.

ii) The transfer of claims from the originator requires the transfer of information regarding borrowers at the time of asset transfer; procedures to effect the transfer should be compatible with Finnish laws concerning privacy and customer protection. The seller should also notify the Financial Supervisory Authorities prior to transfer.

iii) An SPV will be regarded as a "financial institution" rather than a "credit institution", and will thus not be subject to capital adequacy requirements.

iv) The balance sheet of an SPV does not have to be consolidated with that of the originating institution, provided that *a)* the originator does not have the majority of the voting power in the SPV or otherwise control it, and *b)* there are limits on the funding that the originator may provide to the SPV (*i.e.* the originator may not be the main funding source).

v) The transfer of assets to an SPV will be recognised as a "true sale" under Finnish law if: *a)* the originator notifies the borrower at the time of asset transfer (in the future it is possible that a clause authorising such transfers will be contained in standard mortgage documentation); *b)* the originator retains no risk (legal, moral or economic) of loss on the assets that have been securitised, *i.e.* "no recourse", and *c)* the loan transfer is legally valid and the assets are assigned to the SPV.

vi) The removal of assets from the originator's balance sheet will be accepted by bank regulators. Any residual risk will have to be taken into account under rules governing off-balance-sheet commitments. However, any retained equity or subordinated debt position will remain on the books of the originators and will carry the full risk weight applicable to such assets (4 per cent in the case of residential mortgages).

vii) Concerning taxation, there were no special problems identified in cases where the SPV is established outside of Finland. It was however, noted that in cases of domestic SPVs there may be risks of unfavourable tax treatment, if the courts were to decide whether the SPV is engaging in commercial transactions. If the SPV were found not to be engaging in commercial transactions, a less favourable tax regime would apply; the Working Group recommended that a legal ruling on the issue be obtained as soon as possible. It did not appear that the transfer of claims would be subject to stamp duty. However, a Finnish-based SPV would have to pay a credit tax equivalent to 0.5 per cent of the amount of any foreign bond issue; this tax is applied to any foreign loan or bond by entities subject to Finnish domestic taxes; a foreign-based SPV would not be liable for such taxes.

viii) Finland switched from turnover taxation to value-added taxation at the beginning of 1994. Under both systems, credit operations of banks are exempt from taxation, but other operations (*e.g.* trustee, and custodial services) would be liable for such taxes. It appears that servicing by originating banks will be tax-exempt.

ix) The Working Group recommended that regulators should give favourable consideration to investment in asset-backed or mortgage-backed securities by institutional investors, particularly insurance companies.

x) The report noted that the authorities are considering the possibility of extending guarantees for some securitisation-related operations, such as currency swaps, liquidity facilities or subordinated notes.

The authorities have said that while efforts have been made to remove any official impediments to securitisation, the decision of whether to pursue securitisation or alternative techniques to manage their balance sheets rests with the private banks. At this time, Postipankki is seeking to register mortgage-backed securities using Finnish mortgages as collateral with the SEC of the United States, presumably for a placement in the US domestic bond market. Other institutions are reportedly considering similar operations.

France

Securitisation was introduced in France in conjunction with the modernisation of financial markets and banking, a policy that has been in effect since 1983. Major steps in the process have included:

- *i)* creation of the first short-term negotiable debt securities (certificates of deposit) in 1985;
- *ii)* creation of the financial futures market (MATIF) in 1986;
- *iii)* reform of the Treasury bill market and conversion of conventional government debt issues into fungible Treasury bonds (*obligations assimilables du Trésor*, or *OAT*s) in 1986;
- *iv)* establishment of primary dealers in government securities (*spécialistes en valeurs du Trésor*, or *SVT*s) in January 1987;
- *v)* the Stock Market Act of 22 January 1988.

At the same time, undertakings for collective investment in transferable securities (UCITs, which can take the form of SICAVs or FCPs) have been growing rapidly since 1981. In addition, the Act of 24 January 1984 took a first step towards unifying the various legal forms of credit establishments and equivalent institutions, and the prices of bank services began to be deregulated in 1985.

French banks have been showing a growing interest in securitisation, which is seen as an additional tool for managing their balance sheets. The French authorities have, in the past, made a number of statements stressing the importance of securitisation for the competitiveness of French banks, given the freedom of movement for capital and the freedom to provide services within the European Community, as well as broader international competition.

Securitisation can enable French banks to cope better with the mounting constraints of capital adequacy requirements. With a substantial portion of household savings being diverted from current accounts (which pay no interest in France and constitute a special resource for banks) to OPCVMs, banks see securitisation as a means of enhancing liquidity. Moreover, the ratings of several French banks have deteriorated, and securitisation is often considered an effective way of boosting a credit establishment's borrowing capacity and creditworthiness.

Lastly, securitisation was introduced in France in the wake of a major wave of early repayments that began in 1986: from 1986 until 1988, some FF 150 billion in mortgages was renegotiated in one form or another, inflicting heavy losses on credit establishments. In this respect, securitisation is especially important insofar as it has the effect of transferring interest rate risk and the risk of early repayment from credit institutions to financial market investors. All of these features make securitisation, in the same way as derivative securities, an effective tool with which French banks can manage their assets and liabilities.

The French mortgage market is heavily regulated. In France, subsidised housing is traditionally financed by *"Livret A"* passbook savings accounts. First-time homebuyer loans to low-income borrowers are subsidised through the personalised housing benefit (*aide personnalisée au logement*, or APL). The large number of subsidised housing loans, plus the fact that mortgages are a loss-leader for French banks, explain why bank balance sheets show loans that carry very low interest rates. Securitising such receivables is complicated by current market conditions, but declining balances in *Livret A* accounts and, more generally, a lack of long-term savings to finance the French mortgage market have caused a number of specialised housing lenders to see securitisation as a solution to the problem.

In 1992, there was FF 270 billion in outstanding property-backed bonds on the French mortgage market, representing 16 per cent of outstanding mortgages and 9 per cent of outstandings on the national bond market. The only two establishments authorised to issue property-backed bonds, the maturity of which ranges from 10 to 20 years, are Crédit Foncier de France and Caisse de Refinancement Hypothécaire.

Because French legislation differs on many counts from that of the English-speaking countries, securitisation could not be introduced in France by merely importing those countries' models. A special legal framework had to be created, to allow receivables to be transferred (which had traditionally been prohibited), as well as to authorise the creation of trust-like companies (*fidéicommis*). The origins of this framework are found in the "Dailly Act" of 2 January 1981, which made it legal for credit establishments to transfer commercial claims among themselves. But it was the Act of 23 December 1988 and the corresponding decrees that defined the players in the French system of securitisation: securitised loan investment funds (*fonds communs de créances* or FCCs), fund management companies and depositories of receivables. Many provisions of that law were recently amended by the Act of 4 January 1993.

In securitisation, one or more establishments transfer their receivables, as listed on an itemised invoice, to an FCC, and are under no obligation to notify each of the debtors. All of the receivables so acquired must meet uniformity criteria, and none may be in arrears or contested. The structure of capital flows and of interest payable to FCC shareholders is totally unrestricted, thus creating a legal framework that would seem particularly conducive to securitisation.

The entire process is subject to supervision by the stock market regulatory body, the Commission des Opérations de Bourse (COB).

Under the 1988 Act, only credit establishments and the Caisse des Dépôts et Consignations (CDC) were authorised to transfer their receivables. In addition, the term to maturity of those receivables had to exceed two years. FCCs could issue securities corresponding to those receivables only once, and they were prohibited from subsequently acquiring or disposing of receivables.

The rules governing securities issued by FCCs were intended to protect both investors and original debtors. For this reason, investors had to be provided with detailed information, and it was mandatory for FCC securities to be rated. Moreover, credit had to be enhanced in order to shield investors from the risk of debtor delinquency. This enhancement could take the form of an external guarantee by a credit establishment or an insurance company, the FCC could issue securities for less than the total amount of the receivables acquired, or subordinated tranches, with investment restrictions, could be created to bear the entire risk of delinquency. The law also stipulated that the establishment that had made the original loans had to continue to manage those receivables, in order to preserve the rights of the debtors.

The 1988 Act afforded investors special protection against any speculation on the part of FCC issuers by substantially restricting how they could invest the proceeds of their securities. Nevertheless, FCCs were free to invest their cash in Treasury bills or equivalent instruments. In addition, the minimum value of a share was set at FF 10 000 (securitised assets were aimed primarily at credit establishments), and SICAVs affiliated with the transferors of receivables could hold no more than 5 per cent of the securities issued by the corresponding FCCs.

While the French securitisation market seems not to have expanded as rapidly as the most optimistic forecasts for the initial years had projected, some of the first French securitisations were extremely successful (shares issued by the CLFCC90-1 fund on 3 April 1990 sold out in just two days). Some securitisation was carried out simultaneously by agents in France and the United States, with the French agent placing half of an issue with French investors and the American agent placing the other half on the international market.

There are several possible justifications for the fact that auto loans made by DIAC (a financial subsidiary of Renault) were securitised offshore, after the 1988 legislation had been set in place: a lack of familiarity with the new legislation, or fear that the securities could not be placed in the domestic market are likely explanations; it should also be noted that the risk premium tacked onto the initial issues was certainly overestimated by French investors.

From 1988 until April 1993, there were a total of 57 securitisations in France, resulting in aggregate issues of just over FF 33 billion. To date, the mortgage market has seen only one securitisation (in November 1991). It was estimated in 1991 that over FF 650 billion in outstanding housing loans could be securitised.

Most securitisations (40 of them, totalling FF 14 billion) seem to have merely made use of the legislation on FCCs to circumvent French legal requirements that bond issues have maturities of more than seven years. Such securitisations amount to issuing securities backed by a single receivable. These products are aimed primarily at individuals, and their interest rates are more attractive than the returns on conventional savings plans, while their credit risk is extremely slight. They are sold in post offices and have recently become available from commercial banks as well. Their characteristics explain why some observers have referred to them as "false securitisations".

In addition, there have been six securitisations involving a small number of very special receivables. The corresponding issues totalled about FF 5 billion. The receivables in question were claims on stock brokers or local government authorities, or negotiable promissory notes. Issues of this sort have a senior/subordinated structure, and their cost is reduced because of the smaller volume and thus simplified data processing.

Eleven securitisations each bundled a large number of receivables (several thousand), as is common practice on the international market. The corresponding issues totalled FF 14.5 billion. Except for one instance involving mortgages, all related to other sorts of personal loans. Both senior and subordinated tranches were issued, except for two cases (including the most recent) in which credit was enhanced by other forms of guarantees. Each time, the receivables corresponding to the subordinated tranche were kept on the transferor's balance sheet.

Most French securitisations have used the senior/subordinated structure, because, under French law, that is the most economical method of credit enhancement. In legislation passed in August 1989, the Banking Commission ruled that, if a transferor kept the receivables corresponding to an issue's subordinated tranche on its balance sheet, it would have to constitute provisions to cover the risk of debtor delinquency, but the transferor's capital would have to cover only the assets purchased, in contrast to the legislation in force in the United States and the United Kingdom, for example, which requires that capital cover all of the receivables transferred. It can be expected that, on this point, French securitisation law will move towards international norms.

It could be surmised that certain limits imposed by the 1988 legislation helped delay the take-off of securitisation in France. In order to contain consumer credit, the law prohibited the securitisation of short-term assets (of the bank card variety), whereas such assets are the easiest to securitise and offer the highest returns. The fact that FCCs were barred from acquiring additional receivables after their securities were issued limited their lifetimes and made it more expensive to amortise their costs, with profitability suffering as a result. Similarly, the fact that it was illegal to transfer the management of receivables to FCCs caused the high cost of that management, often stemming from a certain administrative inefficiency on the part of credit establishments, to be passed along to FCCs.

The new legislation of 4 January 1993 and the corresponding decrees do away with most of the limits imposed by the original law. Henceforth, the assets of insurance companies may also be securitised. Management companies of FCCs are licensed by the COB, which must also approve the prospectus of any fund that is created. The restriction on the maturity of securitisable receivables will probably be lifted, paving the way for the securitisation of short-term assets. Moreover, FCCs will be given the opportunity to reduce operating costs by subsequently replenishing their receivables and by hedging with interest rate swaps and options. The most recent securitisations in France have made active use of these new possibilities. The new law seems to have made French legislation no more restrictive than that of other countries.

Securitisation in France

(FF million)

Type of receivables securitised	1989-90 No of FCCs	1989-90 Amounts issued	1991 No of FCCs	1991 Amounts issued	1992 No of FCCs	1992 Amounts issued	1993 No of FCCs	1993 Amounts issued	1994 No of FCCs	1994 Amounts issued	Total No of FCCs	Total Amounts issued
Business loans	1	674	1	451	–	–	–	–	–	–	2	1 125
Consumer credit	3	2 471	2	4 215	4	5 178	4	3 880	3	5 293	16	21 037
Interbank loans	3	2 058	17	4 606	22	9 598	24	12 209	21	6 607	87	34 478
Loans to local authorities	1	883	1	704	–	–	1	1 391	–	–	3	2 978
Mortgages	–	–	1	1 000	–	–	–	–	5	8 476	6	9 476
Total	8	6 086	22	10 976	26	14 776	29	17 480	29	19 777		
Running total	8	6 086	30	17 063	56	31 838	85	49 317	114	65 887		
Outstandings	8	5 440	30	15 174	56	25 313	82	36 714	93	46 327		

Source: Observatoire des fonds communs de créances, various issues.

The structure and management capabilities of the French banking system would seem to have impeded the launch of securitisation. Most of the big banks have a highly decentralised commercial network, and local branches generally manage their own receivables. In contrast, securitisation requires centralised management and exact monthly reporting of cash flows. For this reason, the cost of securitisation is initially substantially higher. Subsequently, however, once new computer systems are in place to monitor, control and account for receivables, the cost is considerably reduced. Compagnie Bancaire arranged its fourth securitisation in just four weeks.

It would appear that a nationwide effort to gather and standardize statistical data relating to receivables (*e.g.* loan characteristics, delinquency, early repayment, disputes) still has to be carried out. The lack of statistics is particularly acute in the mortgage market. Filling these gaps should be of great benefit to French securitisation. Aside from facilitating the issuance of securities by FCCs, the availability of such information would make it easier to assess the prices of those securities and cause them to be traded more actively on the secondary market. It would then be possible gradually to set up a liquid national market in securitised assets.

While the growth of securitisation in France may seem somewhat slow, it is nonetheless proceeding at much the same pace as when it first got under way in the United Kingdom. The main obstacles seem closely tied to the information systems, in the broad sense, of credit establishments. While the initial costs are high, there can be no doubt as to the ultimate prospects for securitisation in France. Credit establishments are beginning to fully grasp the advantages, as demonstrated by the fact that newcomers to the market include banks of a far more modest size than the initial transferors.

The recently revamped legal framework seems conducive to the growth of securitisation in France, and French investors are becoming familiar with the products involved. Lower French interest rates, if they continue to ease, will provide substantial impetus for securitisation, of mortgages in particular. In addition, the gradual deregulation of the mortgage market, combined with the shortage of long-term savings in France, will play an important role in promoting securitisation in the coming years.

Germany

In Germany, the origins of asset-related securities date back to the 18th century, when governments and interested landowners developed the idea of using real estate as collateral in raising financial capital in the form of mortgage bonds (*"Hypothekenpfandbriefe"*). In the late 1920s, the communal bond (*"Kommunalobligation"*) was born. Both instruments could only be issued by specialised institutions (see below). Structural characteristics of the German universal banking system, in combination with special regulations for the issue of mortgage and communal bonds, fostered the development of asset-related securitisation at an early stage.

Mortgage and communal bonds are considered safe investments for both retail and institutional investors. The ongoing banking supervision assures that, in addition to the specific pool of mortgages and the claims *vis-à-vis* the public sector, the bank's capital serves as support for all securities. The asset-related securities facilitate the maturity management of the issuing banks through maturity matching. Another characteristic of the German market is the availability of a large volume of mortgage credit, which can be used as collateral to back securities.

Today in Germany, private mortgage banks (which are in many cases majority-owned subsidiaries of commercial banks), public mortgage banks and three "mixed" commercial banks issue mortgage bonds that are secured by mortgages on residential or commercial real estate which the issuing institutions have taken as security. Maturities are usually from 2-10 years, but some maturities are as long as 50 years. A similar asset is the communal bond, the bulk of which is issued in the form of *"Öffentliche Pfandbriefe"*. They are supported by receivables from public sector entities, such as local authorities, Länder Governments, and Federal Government entities. These receivables are predominantly Schuldscheindarlehen (documents which are evidence of interest in a loan). Originally, communal bonds were just a supplementary business to the issue of mortgage bonds, but in recent years the volume of issuance of communal bonds has dwarfed that of mortgage bonds.

In addition to these traditional instruments, commercial banks and specialised financial institutions now issue quite a number of bonds domestically and abroad, via non-resident vehicles, for general funding purposes, including the funding of variable or fixed-rate mortgage lending for residential and commercial real estate. In these cases, the investor is not specifically protected by any direct recourse to collateral. The assets remain on the balance sheet of the originator, as is usually the case with traditional instruments. Without abolishing the specialised regime pertaining to the issue of mortgage and communal bonds, mortgage banks have been authorised to expand the scope of their operations. In 1974 mortgage banks were authorised to issue bonds which are only general obligations of the bank or bonds backed by receivables other than mortgages. Therefore, these securities could not be called *Hypothekenpfandbriefe* or *Öffentliche Pfandbriefe*. Mortgage banks may also now accept, to a limited extent, retail and wholesale deposits for funding. Moreover, mortgage and communal bonds (up to certain limits) can now be issued against receivables from debtors located in other EU countries.

In the case of mortgage and communal bonds, the originating institution keeps the asset on its balance sheet and maintains ultimate responsibility for the credit risk of the bond, while the investor basically assumes all market risks. In effect, the investor is a senior creditor, with payments on the underlying mortgage serving as collateral to guarantee payment of interest and principal; the investor also retains recourse to the issuing institution. Since the originating institution may refuse the prepayment of a loan secured by a mortgage, German *Pfandbriefe* carry no prepayment risk. They also enjoy a high credit quality since mortgage institutions are subject to strict regulatory control over the securities they issue and over their lending activities. In particular, requirements for collateral are very stringent, with the asset pool required to be at least as large as the size of the bond. In addition, mortgage bonds may be used to fund only 60 per cent of the lending value of the pledged property.

The major holders of the assets are banks and retail investors. Insurance companies, investment funds and non-financial corporations are also significant investors. In view of their high credit quality, these assets are treated favourably by the banking regulatory authorities as well as by those responsible for the investments of insurance companies. German pension funds and insurance companies have in the past been restricted by law to certain specified types of investments, including mortgage bonds and communal bonds. However, these restrictions are being lifted in accordance with European Community directives.

The market for asset-related securities offers attractions for all participants. For investors, these assets offer the possibility of obtaining a slightly higher yield than is available on Federal Government bonds, while securing a senior creditor status as well as the guarantee of a major financial institution. Both retail and institutional investors normally seek longer-term assets than banks. These bonds offer the possibility of the institutional investor acquiring assets that, from the maturity viewpoint, match liabilities and, for the retail investor, the possibility of obtaining long-term fixed-income assets. These attractions are a major reason why, in recent years, non-resident institutional investors have likewise started to take a significant interest in mortgage and communal bonds, even though spreads over the yield of Federal Government bonds are rather low and their liquidity much lower than that of Federal Government bonds.

In effect, this form of ''on-balance-sheet securitisation'' results in banks ''unbundling'' the credit risks, which are retained, from the market risks inherent in long-term fixed interest assets, and passing the market risks on to investors. If banks mainly depend upon short-term deposits for funding and have large mortgage portfolios, the risk of maturity mismatches can be serious. Alternatively, banks seeking longer-term assets can purchase them and expand their balance sheets or reshape their maturity profiles. Since the larger German banks, as already mentioned, are also among the major issuers of bonds which are used for general purpose funding, they can act on both sides of the market (*i.e.* as issuers and investors), thereby controlling the size of their balance sheets as well as the maturity structure of assets and liabilities. Thus German banks were able to achieve many of the same benefits, such as limiting interest-rate risk, that are now provided by mortgage-backed securities or by futures, options or interest rate swaps, well before the use of derivatives became common. In more recent times, the availability of swaps has made it possible to add even greater flexibility to this market.

Because the banks are heavily involved in all phases of the asset-related securities market, the German system does not imply the high degree of disintermediation – if narrowly defined in terms of the share of non-securitised bank lending in total lending by the financial system – that characterises some recently developed markets in securitised assets. Thus, this market has enabled the German system of financial intermediation, which remains dominated by universal banks, to gain considerable flexibility and liquidity. At the same time, since the originating institution retains full responsibility for the credit risk of the assets, any loss in the credit standing of the originator will have a direct impact on the marketability of assets.

For all these reasons, asset-related securities play an important role in the German bond market. At the end of 1993, the outstanding volume of all domestic bonds was DM 2 395 billion, leaving aside the amount of DM 319 billion foreign deutschemark bonds. More than one-half of that sum, namely DM 1 316 billion, were bonds issued by banks, among which DM 178 billion were mortgage bonds and DM 573 billion communal bonds (mainly *Öffentliche Pfandbriefe*). The remainder consisted of direct issues by public sector entities, mostly of the Federal government. Domestic corporate bond issues have remained insignificant.

Off-balance-sheet securitisation, as practised in the United States and a few other places, has not progressed very far in Germany. Several characteristics of the German banking system have discouraged this type of securitisation.

It should be stressed that there are no legal impediments to off-balance-sheet securitisation, provided that a true asset sale takes place and that there is no legal recourse on the part of the investors to the originating bank. German civil law allows for special-purpose vehicles owned by a charitable trust to be established, and existing accounting rules enable true asset sales. In addition, assignment of all type of loans is allowed for, without notification to the debtors being required. The Federal Banking Supervisory Office has nevertheless taken an unsympathetic view of such securitisation in the past, questioning in specific cases whether a "true" asset sale was really intended. Another consideration of supervision has been the concern as to whether the true motivation of the originating bank might just constitute a circumvention of supervision.

A further consideration of "moral risk" has been that in cases of solvency and/or liquidity difficulties, the originating bank might feel obliged to buy back the assets in order to protect its own reputation. At any rate, "US-style securitisation" is generally considered in Germany to be riskier than "German-style" securitisation, since asset-backed and mortgage-backed securities do not have the guarantee of the originator.

The most important reasons for the slow progress of off-balance-sheet securitisation have to be sought elsewhere. First, there has been no pressure to use MBS or ABS issuance to reduce the size of balance sheets. The German banking system can be considered to be generally strong and did not go through a period of distress in the 1980s or 1990s. Thus, there has been no particular reason to sell bank assets. German banks' capital/asset ratios have traditionally been adequate. Since German mortgage banks are able to match maturities and interest rates by issuing mortgage bonds and communal bonds, the motivation of avoiding maturity mismatches is also absent. Moreover, the spreads between interest rates on mortgages and interest rates on mortgage bonds have traditionally been very tight. Mortgage banks' net margin over the period between 1981 and 1980 averaged around 75 basis points – compared with an average of 230 basis points net margin for all banks over the same period. On the other hand, concern has arisen among banks that securitisation of assets might jeopardise traditionally close and confidential relationships with customers. Strict rules regarding banking confidentiality in Germany pose formidable obstacles to disclosure in a securitised transaction. In addition, credit margins are lower than in other countries where asset-backed securitisation has developed. Another supply-side reason is the relatively small volume of consumer loans. Some banks active in this area may de facto be specialised consumer finance institutions. All the same, these institutions have general banking licences. At any rate, they have no particular difficulties in refinancing themselves "on-balance-sheet", within the domestic banking system or elsewhere.

The demand for the ABS and MBS types of securities seems to be quite moderate. German investors continue to be rather conservative. The importance of institutional investors is comparatively small in comparison with the US market. This is not due to any lack of sophistication, but rather to structural features of the economy. For instance, owing to the prevailing public nature of German pension systems, private pension funds are far less important than in the United States.

No public issue of a bank-originated mortgage-backed security has achieved domestic off-balance-sheet financing in Germany. Nevertheless, there has been one true off-balance-sheet asset-backed securitised deal to date. The DM 230 million deal was entered into in December 1990 for KKB Bank AG, an affiliate of Citibank. The transaction, involving an offshore Special Purpose Vehicle, was structured as a syndicated loan which was placed privately. The issued securities were backed by consumer loans. Moreover, although they did not receive off-balance-sheet treatment, a few deutschemark-denominated securitised deals, such as the DM 100 million operation by Europäische Hypothekenbank in February 1990, have been attempts to repackage a number of *Pfandbriefe* using an offshore SPV.

There is some scope for the securitisation of receivables other than those originated by banks. Typically, auto loans and leases are granted in Germany by financial subsidiaries of car manufacturers that are called "auto banks". Although being de facto specialised institutions, they are treated as universal banks under German Law. Autobanks have shown a growing interest in securitisation, which is seen as a potential tool for asset and liability management as well as a potential means of funding. In addition, there have been a few consumer loan securitised deals by affiliates of foreign banks and a few auto loan deals. Some auto loan transactions have been swapped into US dollars and placed in the American market.

Taking all factors together, there may be some scope for off-balance-sheet securitisation in market niches, but no general transformation of the German financial system in this respect can be envisaged for some time to come. In the end, competition will determine the viability of individual financial instruments.

Italy

Despite the very high potential for securitisation offered by mortgage and car markets, the spread of domestic securitisation in Italy is basically hindered by the lack of a specific legislative and regulatory framework providing uniform rules for this type of operation.

Three kinds of problems pose obstacles to securitisation deals in Italy, notably:

  i) the limits imposed on financial intermediaries on the issuance of so-called atypical securities;

  ii) debtor notification requirements – in the case of the transfer of outstanding credit;

  iii) the slightly unfavourable fiscal treatment *vis-à-vis* other forms of investments.

As regards point *i)*, the civil code, which limits bond issues to the amount of the issuer's equity capital, is supplemented by the rules embodied in the resolution of 3 March 1994 of the Interministerial Committee for Credit and Savings, implementing Article 11 of the 1993 Banking Law (Legislative Decree 385 of 1 September 1993). For companies whose shares are listed in regulated markets and for the financial companies listed in the special register envisaged by Article 107 of the Banking Law, the resolution raises the limit to the sum of paid-up capital and reserves.

This ceiling applies both to bonds and to other debt securities (''financial paper'', envisaged by Law 43 of 13 January 1994, and ''investment certificates'', envisaged by the Credit Committee resolution of 3 March 1994).

As to instruments different from typical securities, the Credit Committee resolution of 12 January 1994 implementing Article 129 of the Banking Law provides that the Bank of Italy may block the execution of operations when the instruments involved are not envisaged by the regulations and not in sufficiently common use, and thus cannot be fitted into a generally applicable model that is promoted or handled by securities market intermediaries subject to prudential supervision and agreed with the supervisory authorities.

As to problem *ii)*, the enactment of Law 52/91 was seen as a first step towards the creation of the legal framework necessary for securitisation. Companies operating in this field were exempted from debtor notification requirements. Furthermore, that law stated the principle of the irrevocable nature of the sale of credits by companies operating under this law.

As regards problem *iii)*, tax rates on national and international bonds are uniform at 12.5 per cent on all new issues while the rate on atypical securities is 15 per cent. Another tax problem arises from provisions under which sale of receivables for financing purposes to an offshore company outside Italy is subject to a tax of 15 per cent. This tends to make securitisation more costly than other forms of financing.

Finally, the off-balance-sheet treatment of securitised assets and the risk weightings that will be assigned to asset-backed and mortgage-backed securities held by banks are currently being discussed in international fora where Italian delegations are making their own contributions. Italy will accordingly adopt the rules that are jointly decided.

Japan

At this time, relatively little domestic securitisation has taken place in Japan in spite of recent progress toward setting up the required legal and regulatory infrastructure. At the same time, the Japanese investor community is very large, with a strong demand for attractive assets. Japanese investors are already major purchasers of MBS and ABS originated in other markets. Moreover, Japanese financial intermediaries have considerable experience in operating in securitised markets outside of Japan. There is also considerable cross-border issuance of asset-backed commercial paper taking place by Japanese banks and non-financial corporations.

Under the traditional financial system, some possibility existed to trade mortgage-related claims but only a small amount of trading has in fact occurred, reflecting limited desire to securitise assets. Some capacity exists to sell mortgage deeds or mortgage certificates; residential mortgage trusts exist under which pools of residential mortgages can be sold, subject to requirements to notify the borrowers. The main sellers of such assets are city banks, other banks, housing loan companies and mortgage companies. The main purchasers are the banks, some specialised finance institutions and insurance companies. Although some capacity to trade such assets has existed since the early 1970s, it is estimated that only about 1 per cent of mortgages are actually ever traded.

An important factor that has inhibited progress toward off-balance-sheet securitisation to date seems to be strong concern, especially among banks, that securitisation may erode traditionally close ties between banks and their corporate customers, which has long been a defining feature of the Japanese financial system as well as of the country's system of corporate governance.

With these underlying factors encouraging key players to proceed with great caution, some progress has been made in adapting the infrastructure to allow some form of securitisation, but there remain several issues in the Japanese legal framework.

In Japan, ABS and MBS are not legally recognised as securities. The Securities Exchange Law (SEL) of 1948 contained a list of specific instruments recognised as securities which covered the range of instruments existing at the time. The list has been subsequently lengthened by revision of the law and the cabinet can also designate new kinds of securities by issuing an order. (See below.) However, ABS and MBS are not fully officially designated as securities. Financial institutions could still apply to the Finance Ministry for approval to trade such instruments without their being designated securities, but in that case lesser rules governing investor protection would apply and possibilities to market such instruments would be narrower.

An additional issue is the Civil Code which stipulates that, in order for a transfer of an asset to be recognised, the individual borrower must be notified. This would make the transfer of claims on large number of borrowers, such as pools of mortgage loans and consumer credits, rather cumbersome.

As the global phenomenon of securitisation gained in importance in the 1980s, a certain amount of securitisation-related activity has occurred. Thus, Citibank has launched several important deals. In 1990, a programme was begun to sell trade receivables from Kawasaki Steel to a US-based SPV as the basis for a dollar-denominated commercial paper programme to be distributed to US investors. Later in 1990, Citibank developed another asset-backed CP programme based upon consumer receivables from Daiei Finance, a major consumer finance company. Other commercial paper programmes have been undertaken for other companies by foreign banks. Similarly, the main Japanese banks have sponsored multi-seller asset-backed CP programmes in the United States. Under these programmes, Japanese corporate borrowers usually sell their yen receivables to an SPV in the United States. The receivables are swapped into dollars and sold to United States investors. At the same time, Citibank has marketed to investors in Japan tranches of its global CP programme backed by credit card receivables originated outside Japan.

The authorities have been giving increasing consideration to modifying the legal and institutional system so as to allow domestic institutions to expand their range of activities. In March 1990, the Ministry of Finance permitted banks to sell loans on a ''whole loan'' basis. In the period ending March 31, 1993, loan sales had amounted to 2.3 trillion yen ($20 billion). These loan sales have been carried out by using loan transfer schemes rather than securitisation. Most sales have been by city banks, with the major buyers being regional banks, insurance companies and foreign banks. Foreign banks (especially European banks) have been particularly large buyers of loans. The foreign banks purchased loans at favourable prices and in some cases hoped to use loans thus purchased to build relationships with Japanese corporate customers.

In 1991, two advisory bodies to the Ministry of Finance, the Financial System Research Council and the Securities and Exchange Council, undertook studies in order to make recommendations concerning needed structural changes in the financial system. The studies recommended that a new definition of securities in Japan should be established, taking into consideration those of other major markets, and that the authorities consider the modification of the SEL to cover foreign ABS and MBS, mainly for investor protection purposes.

Possibly in response to these recommendations, the authorities decided to adopt a gradual and cautious approach, which will make it possible to issue MBS and ABS in specialised markets where large financial institutions and investors are predominant. Once it is determined whether market participants desire to undertake large-scale securitisation, consideration may be given to further modifications in legal and regulatory structures. In 1992 the Diet approved certain changes to the laws. In particular, the list of recognised securities was lengthened to include: a) promissory notes issued by juridical persons for funding purposes, and b) securities or certificates issued by foreign juridical persons which represent beneficiary trust interests in a pool of receivables arising from loans by banking or lending institutions or similar interests designated by the Ministry of Finance. In addition, some claims, whether or not evidenced by physical certificates, were designated as securities, including: *a)* rights in trusts of loans by banks, trust companies or other financial institutions primarily engaged in long-term lending for housing and real estate, and *b)* similar rights in assets held by foreign legal entities. As before, the law allows for other securities to be recognised upon issuance of a cabinet order and foreign certificates of deposit (CDs) have been so designated using this provision. In general the law has been interpreted as adding to the list of securities: *a)* commercial paper; *b)* housing loan trust certificates, and *c)* foreign-originated and held assets using bank-originated receivables as eligible collateral. Having been designated as securities, these instruments are subject to disclosure requirements under MOF regulations. The rules on private placements were also changed to allow for exemptions from disclosure requirements in cases where securities are placed with less than 50 investors (previously the threshold between private and public offerings).

Shortly after these amendments to the SEL were enacted, a Law for the Regulation of Business Related to Specified Claims (the Specified Claims Law) was passed. This law, which came into full effect in June 1993, placed responsibility for supervision of companies originating certain categories of claims, including leases, credit card receivables and other consumer credits made by non-bank institutions under the ministry of Trade and Industry (MITI) and the MOF. In the past, lease companies and non-bank finance companies obtained funding mainly from bank credit; this law would allow them to diversify funding. The law also placed responsibility for the setting of rules covering the assignment of lease assets to MITI and MOF. In general this law has made it easier for originators to assign assets covered by the law without notifying individual debtors. Instead, notification might take the form of announcements in newspapers or similar methods. In order to use such methods, originators must submit a plan to MITI for confirmation before implementation.

The law, which was aimed at protecting investors with regard to assignment of lease claims, also created some new uncertainties. Thus, it was left unclear the conditions under which an assignment of assets would be considered a ''true sale'' rather than a financing. Market participants have noted that the law still leaves great discretion to the ministries in accepting or rejecting various categories of collateral and various structures for securities. The law allows for the creation of special-purpose companies but leaves it unclear whether such companies will be given bankruptcy-remote status. Similarly, the tax liability of various kinds of operations needed to effect securitisation is uncertain. In any event, an asset created under its provisions is not automatically recognised as a security under SEL and therefore its marketability will be limited. On balance this law makes certain operations necessary for securitisation easier.

In June 1993, the Diet approved an amendment to Article 297 of the Commercial Code which eliminated the ceiling on corporate bond issuance and made it easier for companies with small net assets to issue debt. This law would permit SPVs to issue securities if SPVs were recognised as corporations authorised under the commercial code. However, it is not clear whether such SPVs would be subject to double taxation.

On 16 September 1994, the possibilities to engage in securitisation were broadened when the Ministry of Finance and the Ministry of Trade and Industry issued a ruling under the Specified Claims Law, which also modified the Securities and Exchange Law, the Foreign Securities Company Law and the Foreign Exchange Law. Under the new regulations, receivables of a resident lease company or credit card company (*i.e.* specified claims) may be consolidated into pools which can be sold to offshore SPVs. Investment banks will be able to repackage the collateral for resale as ''claim notes'' which may be denominated in yen or in foreign currency. The Claim Notes will not be fully recognised as securities and thus will not be available to the general investing public in Japan; nor will they have the full support of domestic investor protection systems. These assets may be sold by non-resident securities houses to non-resident investors. After a 90-day ''seasoning'' period these assets may be sold in denominations of at least ¥ 50 million to those resident financial institutions which are authorised to deal with foreign securities houses (*i.e.* banks, trust companies or insurance companies, etc.) but may not be sold to Japanese securities companies or to Japanese branches of foreign securities houses. Such assets may also be traded in the secondary market, but Japanese securities houses and Japanese branches of foreign securities houses may not engage in secondary market trading. In keeping with the policy of gradually considering expanding the scope for securitisation, the authorities will try to ascertain the strength of investor demand for these new assets before considering further measures to make securitisation possible.

In summary, prospects for large-scale securitisation remain uncertain. It is especially uncertain whether market participants would begin large-scale domestic securitisation, even if the needed legal and regulatory frameworks were established. At the same time, the MOF continues to study the situation. On 25 November 1993, the Ministry of Finance organised a working group within the Banking Bureau to study the possibilities for expanded asset sales as well as to address remaining problems regarding asset securitisation. The group will reportedly consider the possibility to sell assets such as commercial loans, automobile loans made by finance companies and corporate receivables. Participants hope that some useful recommendations will be offered in relation to securitisation in the course of the future.

Netherlands

The Dutch mortgage market, which amounted to Gld 245 billion in March 1994, is among the largest in Europe. Dutch banks may extend mortgage loans for up to 125 per cent of the execution value (*i.e.* the auction value) of a residential property. Since the execution value is normally 60-80 per cent of the free market value, the mortgage can be for 75-100 per cent of the market value. In the past, when mortgages were sometimes guaranteed by a municipality, the loan could be for 100 per cent of free market value. From January 1995 on, for new issued mortgages the guarantees of the municipalities will be replaced by guarantees of a fund, which will be financed by premiums paid by the persons asking for a guarantee. There is no reason to expect that banks will treat those guaranteed mortgages differently from mortgages guaranteed by the municipalities. Mortgages can be at fixed or variable interest rates. Commercial banks traditionally play the largest part in this market. In 1992, banks accounted for some 62 per cent of all mortgages. Specialised mortgage institutions (mortgage banks and building societies) are traditionally important providers of mortgage finance, and accounted for nearly 25 per cent of all new mortgages in 1993. Moreover, the distinction between mortgage banks and other institutions have largely been eliminated. In some cases mortgage institutions have lost market share to other intermediaries or in other cases the mortgage institutions have become parts of larger financial conglomerates. Other institutions (particularly insurance companies and pension funds) supply the remainder.

There exists in the Netherlands a special mortgage bond (*Pandbrief*) which may be issued only by mortgage banks and which remains on the issuer's balance sheet. The holder of mortgage bonds has no particular claim over a given pool of mortgage assets and has recourse only to the issuing institution. With the decline of the importance of mortgage banks, the volume of the mortgage bonds market is rather small; it amounted to Gld 4.9 billion in 1991 – only about 2 per cent of outstanding mortgage loans. Another factor causing contraction in the *Pandbrief* market has been the removal of certain fiscal advantages for this instrument.

Although the practice of holding sizeable portfolios of mortgages creates a potential maturity mismatch, the banks have numerous tools to deal with the problem. In particular, banks issue *Bankbrieven*, bonds which are similar to the *Pandbrieven* issued by the mortgage banks, and banks also receive term deposits, especially from institutional investors. Sales of mortgages in whole-loan form to investors also assist in reducing mismatches.

There have been no public off-balance-sheet mortgage-backed or asset-backed securitisations to date in The Netherlands. However, the domestic market has seen certain private placements backed by assets (especially mortgages). The Rabobank, the NMB-Bank and the Westland Utrecht Hypotheekbank have sold mortgage portfolios to the Algemeen Burgerlijk *pensioenfonds*. However, the mortgage sales were sold directly and not transformed into marketable securities. Other pension funds reportedly may be interested in buying mortgage-related assets. Furthermore, in late 1993, a Dutch insurance company announced the creation of a collective investment instrument to invest in mortgages which will be purchased from institutional investors. If similar operations were to ensue, the secondary market in mortgage-related paper would become more active.

At this time, there is no economic force impelling Dutch institutions to begin large-scale securitisation. The Netherlands have a well-established and liberalised capital market and the secondary market is liquid. The Dutch banks' capital ratios are adequate. As mentioned above, Dutch banks have evolved alternative means of achieving many of the objectives that are reached through securitisation. Thus, interest rate mismatches can be minimised since banks fund themselves through medium to long-term loans granted by insurance funds and pension funds – Dutch pension funds are among the largest in the world. Additionally, because of the traditionally low spreads paid by major Dutch corporates on straight debt, there is no significant funding advantage (from the borrowers' side) of a securitised issue. Another reason for the low interest in issuing mortgage-backed securities in the Netherlands is that spreads of mortgage rates over government bond rates are very low, and therefore MBS would not be very attractive to investors.

Although the main explanation for the negligible level of securitisation is lack of demand by market participants, there are also some uncertainties concerning the capacity of the financial infrastructure in the Netherlands to support securitisation. Under the new Dutch Civil Code, dated 1992, transfer of a loan cannot be achieved without the debtor being notified. Uncertainty remains as to whether the law will recognise the bankruptcy-remote status of an SPV. The Securities Law of 1992 would probably recognise securities issued through securitisation. Dutch accounting standards are very advanced, but it is still uncertain whether the supervisory authorities will accept off-balance-sheet treatment of sold assets. Dutch mortgages are not highly standardized, which could slow the creation of an MBS market, but the fact that a significant number of mortgages have been transferred among institutions suggests that this problem is manageable. Problems of infrastructure do not appear to be very serious and could probably be addressed rather swiftly if a desire to undertake large-scale securitisation were to appear.

Somewhat paradoxically, a few securitised transactions originating in other countries have been issued using Dutch-based SPVs, most probably because no withholding taxes are levied on interest earned by offshore companies.

New Zealand

Both the ABS and the MBS markets remain rather small, although the legal and regulatory framework would apparently permit wider securitisation if demand were sufficient. The small size of the domestic financial system and the relatively strong positions of the banks impede faster expansion. Market participants find securitisation programmes to be rather costly to establish, especially in view of the small amount of business. Furthermore, tight interest rate margins have impeded securitisation.

Most mortgages in New Zealand are 20 years in maturity. About 95 per cent of mortgages are floating-rate instruments with rates reset periodically, with one to three months' notice. The registered banks are the main providers of new mortgage finance. The Housing Corporation of New Zealand (HCNZ) was formerly active in the market and still has about NZ$ 2 billion in mortgages on its books, but is no longer writing substantial amounts of new loans. There is now only one building society of significant size, the Southland Building Society. Thus, building societies no longer are main suppliers of mortgage finance. Loan-to-value ratios of 70 per cent are typical, but some banks will lend up to 90 per cent of valuation with insurance.

A number of MBS have been issued, but total volume is believed to be less than NZ$ 1 billion. Most issues have been privately placed and trading is very thin. In 1989, the first publicly issued MBS of some NZ$ 200 million originated by the United Building Society was marketed in the US dollar euro-bond market and swapped into New Zealand dollars. In 1990, a domestic "pass-through" security originated by ANZ bank was launched with several banks and insurance companies providing credit enhancement and liquidity facilities.

In 1992, one major deal of approximately NZ$ 275 billion occurred. A pool of 11 000 residential mortgages from the HCNZ was sold to a special-purpose company which used a series of credit enhancements and liquidity facilities. The company also used a series of swaps to transform cash flows from floating mortgage payments into fixed-rate payments so as to match commitments to investors.

The ABS market is even smaller than the MBS market. Market observers report that the only ABS deal to date was a Farmers Consumer Credit securitisation of credit card receivables (approximately NZ$ 150 million).

In none of these operations were any major obstacles from legal or regulatory structures identified. The main factors inhibiting growth appear to be the small size of the market and the relatively strong position of the banks. Investors would probably respond favourably to well-rated securities offering a yield pick-up over government securities. Under the Reserve Bank of New Zealand's capital adequacy framework, MBS are assigned a risk weighting of 50 per cent, provided the risks, claims, interests, rights and rewards associated with the underlying mortgages are transferred to the holder of the security. When securities are backed by more than one type of asset, the entire issue is assigned the risk weighting applicable to the asset with the highest risk weighting.

Norway

Norway has a well-developed system of mortgage finance, characterised by on-balance-sheet lending and a market in mortgage bonds. An acute banking crisis in the late 1980s and early 1990s left most of the major banks in need of government support. At this time the authorities are considering techniques other than off-balance-sheet securitisation to deal with the problems of the financial system.

Through the mid-1980s, the financial system was highly regulated and numerous restrictions were imposed on international capital movements. Commercial and savings banks were the dominant institutions in the credit market, and state banks were also significant. Furthermore, each category of institution faced restraints on the kinds of activities it could undertake. Since the mid-1980s, considerable blurring of functions has occurred.

Mortgage institutions do not have a dominant role in lending for residential housing. Thus, in 1991, mortgage institutions accounted for about 10 per cent of personal housing loans, with commercial banks, state banks, savings banks and life insurance companies each having larger shares. (Since the banking crisis, some 90 per cent of the financing of new residential housing has been provided by the State Housing Bank.) At the same time, mortgage institutions accounted for about 24 per cent of loans to trade and industry (wholesale trade and commission broking, retail trade and industry).

Residential mortgages offered by mortgage institutions are long (up to 35 years) with interest rates normally reset at one-, three- or five-year intervals. Borrowers may repay loans at the time of resetting, but prepayment at other times is subject to penalties. Banks have tended to grant variable-rate loans.

There were 14 private mortgage institutions until 1991. Some of the mortgage banks are specialised (fisheries, shipping, etc.), but others engage in general commercial and consumer lending. Most mortgage institutions are specialised companies owned by small groups of banks, insurance companies or pension funds. The distinctive feature of the mortgage institutions is that they are limited to secured lending and are the only institutions that may issue mortgage bonds (*kredittforetaksobligasjon*), *i.e.* bonds which are secured by mortgages or with a guarantee from the government or another financial institution. Other institutions such as banks may issue similarly secured bonds, but only the mortgage banks use the title ''mortgage bonds''.

In 1991, mortgage institutions accounted for about 14 per cent of total lending. The collateral which backs mortgage bonds can be residential mortgages (up to 80 per cent of valuation) or mortgages on machinery and equipment (up to 50 per cent of valuation). The maturity of loans is supposed to be limited to the useful life of the assets being financed.

The mortgage banks obtain the bulk of their financing by issuing medium-term fixed-rate mortgage bonds. Among credit institutions, only the mortgage institutions and the state banks have traditionally used bond issues as a funding technique, although with the deregulation of financial activity since 1985, banks have begun to issue bonds as well. In 1991, bonds issued by mortgage institutions accounted for about 30 per cent of total bonds outstanding, and constituted the largest single category of bonds. By the second quarter of 1993, the per centage had been halved and mortgage bonds now represent the second largest category (smaller than government bonds). It is estimated that secured bonds (*i.e.* all bonds of the mortgage banks and similar bonds issued by other institutions) comprise more than half of the total bond market.

Mortgage bonds give the investor a preferred status *vis-à-vis* other creditors. Because of their higher degree of security, mortgage bonds are seen as the second most secure category of bonds after government and government-guaranteed bonds, and are among the most liquid instruments.

Mortgage bonds, which usually have maturities of two to five years, may be publicly offered or privately placed. If they are publicly offered, they have to be launched through broker firms which may market an entire issue or may form a consortium. Mortgage bonds are in tap-offered bullet form, paying fixed coupon interest and with maturities of up to five years. New bonds may be issued within a series up to one year before maturity. Publicly offered bonds are listed on the Oslo Stock Exchange. Trading which now mainly takes place by telephone is maintained by banks and brokerage houses. Some issues are highly liquid. The trend has been to make smaller numbers of large-sized issues to improve liquidity. Among the purchasers of mortgage securities are the National Insurance Fund (Pension Fund), Norges Postbank, mortgage institutions, banks, insurance companies and collective investment funds.

The mortgage bonds are used to fund the mortgage banks' lending portfolios, which are generally of longer average maturity than those of other institutions. There is no requirement that assets and liabilities be perfectly matched, and some institutions may seek to make profits by ''gapping'' their position. Institutions may also issue short-term securities called ''certificates'' for funding purposes. The large funding mismatches that occurred in the late 1980s and early 1990s contributed to the sharp deterioration in the creditworthiness of financial institutions.

Before the banking crisis that began in 1990, the yield on mortgage bonds was about 10 basis points above that of a comparable benchmark government issue. With the deterioration of credit quality, the spreads increased substantially for some years. However, they are now below the pre-banking-crisis level.

The banking crisis has led to considerable additional changes in activities by various categories of institution. Government support for the banking system has been heavy; total support by the government and central bank to the commercial and savings banks and the savings bank Guarantee Fund amounted to about 24 billion Norwegian kroner in the period 1988-92, which constitutes 3.4 per cent of GDP in 1992. As a consequence, the state has become majority owner of the three largest commercial banks. While a few mortgage institutions suffered severe credit losses and two institutions failed, the mortgage institutions generally survived the crisis better than the commercial banks. Still, the mortgage institutions have come under some pressure since they have experienced a decline in the value of collateral and now will be obliged to observe BIS capital norms. Reflecting these factors, some mortgage institutions have applied for full banking licenses which will enable them to diversify both funding sources and lending activities. Some financial institutions that were organised as mutual credit associations have been transformed into joint stock companies, partly in order to be able to access the equity market for recapitalisation and, by having been granted an ordinary banking licence, to be included in the safety net for banks. Other mortgage institutions have been acquired by banks and incorporated into financial conglomerates. After the support measures to the banking system were scaled down to zero through 1993, there are signs that the process of transformation to banks is slowing down or may be stopping.

Despite the crisis in the banking sector, the authorities do not appear to have given consideration to off-balance-sheet securitisation as a means of dealing with the problems of the banking system; nor has any of the major financial institutions. It would probably be legally possible to sell domestic receivables into an offshore SPV, but this may require authorisation from the Ministry of Finance.

Spain

Since January 1986 when Spain joined the European Community, significant measures have been taken to modernise and liberalise the financial system. Some of the most important include the following:

- implementation of measures to create a deep and liquid government bond market;
- reorganisation of the equity market;
- creation of financial futures and options markets; and
- removal of limitations regarding payment of interests on deposits.

Although Spanish banks' capital-asset ratios are healthy, banks are becoming more interested in securitisation. Unit trusts which invest in money market instruments have eroded the Spanish banks' access to easy liquidity. Securitisation therefore can be a cost-effective source of long-term funds.

Spanish mortgages, the majority of which are held by the regional savings banks (*cajas de ahorro*), are increasingly floating-rate instruments with a term of fifteen years. Mortgages only exceptionally exceed 80 per cent of the assessed value of the property. If the credit institution issues mortgage certificates, the limit is set by law at 70 per cent (80 per cent for residential mortgages). Since the early 1980s the Spanish Government has been promoting the development of a market in mortgage-related assets as a means of lowering housing costs.

Traditionally, the transferability of Spanish mortgages was limited by a high degree of decentralisation of the savings banks as well as by heavy stamp duties. As a result, appropriate mortgage-related instruments had to be developed to make the transfer of economic ownership of mortgages possible. In the early 1980s, mortgage lenders were allowed to issue three types of new mortgage securities: *cedulas hipotecarias, bonos hipotecarios*, and *participaciones hipotecarias*. "Cedulas hipotecarias" are secured by the issuing institution's whole portfolio of eligible mortgage loans, with the exception of those loans that are used to secure issues of *bonos* or those that are sold as *participaciones* and subject to extensive and costly formalities. *Participaciones hipotecarias*, on the other hand, represent shares in a specific mortgage loan (rather than a mortgage pool). *Bonos hipotecarios*, an instrument combining some features of the other two mortgage-related instruments, represent a share in a specific pool of mortgage loans. At the same time, some strict requirements for issues of *bonos* were imposed. A notice must be placed in the Public Property Register detailing all mortgaged properties in the pool. The issue must be recorded in a Public Notice and an association of investors in the issue must be established. All of these requirements make the issue of bonos hipotecarios rather cumbersome. Institutions issuing these mortgage-related instruments retain the mortgages on their balance sheets. In addition, the law of 25 March 1981 created a new kind of specialised mortgage institution, the Sociedad de Credito Hipotecario.

Despite this official support, the Spanish mortgage bond market did not attain very large proportions, with a total Ptas 800 billion mortgage bonds outstanding in 1993 which was equal to 8 per cent of the mortgage market whereas the domestic bond market amounted to Ptas 10 700 billion. Consequently, it was decided to create a legal framework for off-balance-sheet securitisation of mortgage assets. However, the existing complex legal requirements for the registration and transfer of a loan as well as the lack of a "trust" concept made it impossible simply to introduce the international securitisation market into Spain. Thus, specific mechanisms compatible with the Spanish legal system had to be devised.

The first step towards securitisation was made with Royal Decree 1289/1991, which allowed for off-balance-sheet treatment of assets secured by mortgage certificates – particularly *participationes hypotecarias* – when these certificates were sold to investors, either directly or through an SPV. (In fact, all MBS in Spain have used *participaciones hipotecarias* as collateral.) In order to qualify for off-balance-sheet treatment *participaciones hipotecarias* must be sold to the investors up to maturity. However, even though fully-fledged off-balance sheet securitisation through issuance of bonds by an SPV was made possible, the legal nature and bankrupty-remoteness of Spanish issuing vehicles were still uncertain. These legal uncertainties as well as expectations of further modifications of the law seem to have been among the main reasons why the mortgage securitisation market virtually stopped growing after only three operations were completed in 1991.

A further step was taken on 7 July 1992 with the creation of a specific legal framework for securitisation of mortgage assets, under which *participaciones hipotecarias* can be sold to a *fondo de titulizacion*, which is a bankruptcy-remote structure for securitisations. Initially, only securitisation of mortgage assets was made possible through that structure. However, an amendment to the law was passed on 2 March 1993 which extended the coverage to credit, leasing and other types of receivables.

Fondos must be administered by specific management companies called *gestoras*. Five *gestoras* have been so far established, three of which have foreign participation. In addition, the securities issued by the *fondos* have to be rated by an independent, recognised rating agency.

Under Law 19/1992 on securitisation, the assets backing the mortgage certificates sold to a *fondo* are taken off the balance sheet of the originator. Criteria governing the risk weightings for credit institutions holding the bonds as assets were enunciated by the Ministry of Finance. The Securities Commission (Comision Nacional del Mercado de Valores) analyses each issue; the issue is assigned a 50 per cent risk weighting if the underlying loans are secured by mortgages on residential property which will be occupied or offered for rent by the borrower; otherwise the issue is assigned a 100 per cent risk weighting. The Bank of Spain assures that "participaciones hipotecarias" meet the requirement needed for removal from the balance sheet of the originator.

Securitisations to date in Spain

1990	Type of assets	=	Auto receivables
	Amount of the issue	=	Ptas 7 billion
	Issuer	=	Spanish subsidiary of Citibank
1991	Type of assets	=	Mortgages cash flows
	Amount of the issue	=	Ptas 1.5 billion
	Issuer	=	Banco Bilbao Vizcaya
1991	Type of assets	=	Interests in a mortgage participation pool
	Amount of the issue	=	Ptas 7 billion
	Issuer	=	Citibank España
October 1991	Type of assets	=	Participaciones hipotecarias
	Amount of the issue	=	Ptas 12.75 billion
	Issuer	=	Hipotebanco SA
11 January 1993	Type of asset	=	Unsecured corporate loans
	Amount of the issue	=	$1 billion Eurocommercial Paper Programme
	Issuer	=	Banesto
July 1993	Type of asset	=	Participaciones hipotecarias
	Amount of the issue	=	Ptas 13.5 billion
	Issuer	=	Hipotebansa I (Banco de Santander)
September 1993	Type of asset	=	Participaciones hipotecarias
	Amount of the issue	=	Ptas 11.5 billion
	Issuer	=	Banco Hipotecario de España S.A.
November 1993	Type of asset	=	Participaciones hipotecarias
	Amount of the issue	=	Ptas 2.85 billion
	Issuer	=	AIG Finanzas I
December 1993	Type of asset	=	Participaciones hipotecarias
	Amount of the issue	=	Ptas 12 billion
	Issuer	=	Ibercaja (50%), CA Mediterraneo (25%), CAM de Burgos (25%)
January 1994	Type of asset	=	Participaciones hipotecarias
	Amount of the issue	=	Ptas 16 billion
	Issuer	=	Hipotebansa II (Banco de Santander)
June 1994	Type of asset	=	Participaciones hipotecarias
	Amount of the issue	=	Ptas 45 billion
	Issuer	=	Hipotebansa III (Banco de Santander)
November 1994	Type of asset	=	Participaciones hipotecarias
	Amount of the issue	=	Ptas 10.45 billion
	Issuer	=	UCI 1, Unión de Créditos, Hipotecarios SA, Entidad de Financiación
November 1994	Type of asset	=	Participaciones hipotecarias
	Amount of the issue	=	Ptas 10 billion
	Issuer	=	C Gral. A. Granada (60%), C.A. Castilla-La Mancha (40%)

Source: IFR, International Securitisation Report, various issues.

Until recently, the Spanish authorities have focused on developing mechanisms to securitise residential mortgages and there had not been strong incentives to securitise non-mortgage assets. Nevertheless, on 11 January 1993, Banco Espannol de Crédito (Banesto) became the first continental European bank to remove corporate loans from its balance sheet which had been used to support issuance of asset-backed euro-commercial paper. These developments demonstrate the high level of interest in securitisation in Spain, despite the comparatively low volume of activity to date. Furthermore, on 14 April 1994, a law was enacted enabling the authorities to regulate the securitisation of assets other than mortgages.

The Spanish authorities as well as most market participants believe that following recent modifications, the Spanish legal and accounting systems are adequate to permit the advance of securitisation. Nevertheless, some problems with infrastructure may still persist. It is reported that disclosure and presentation requirements for the listing of securities make it difficult to obtain regulatory approval for the issue of mortgage-backed or asset-backed securities. Additionally, a 25 per cent withholding tax is imposed on interest payments for which foreign investors have considerable difficulty in obtaining reimbursement.

Sweden

Sweden has a well-developed market in conventional mortgage bonds, as well as significant recent experience with off-balance sheet securitisation. Future use of off-balance sheet securitisation may lead to structural change in the mortgage sector. Moreover, securitisation may be used in the present process of restoring the soundness of the banking system.

Although mortgage banking has been present in Sweden since the early 19th century, the system in its present form dates from the early 1960s. Mortgages are traditionally granted for rather long periods. Since the capacity of commercial banks to lend for more than one year is limited by law, several other categories of institution are also active in housing finance. Most long-term lending is provided by the mortgage institutions, most of which are specialised subsidiaries of banks; one of the largest, however, is government-owned. Insurance companies are also to some extent engaged in direct housing finance.

A borrower may obtain housing credit from more than one of these institutions simultaneously, at differing interest rates, to finance the same property. Thus mortgage institutions will normally extend loans for a maximum of 75-85 per cent of assessed valuation while other institutions (*e.g.* banks) may lend for the portion of financing that exceeds this percentage.

Interest rates tend to be fixed for a period of generally two or five years, after which the rate is reset. The borrower may repay the loan at the end of the period, but prepayment is generally not permitted at other times. Some banks and finance companies have also offered floating-rate mortgages. In addition to residential mortgages, financial institutions (*e.g.* banks, mortgage institutions, insurance companies and finance companies and specialised institutions) offer similar secured loans to finance commercial real estate, agricultural property, construction and maritime shipping. Some mortgage institutions specialise in financing these activities rather than residential real estate.

Mortgage institutions fund themselves mainly by issuing mortgage bonds, which account for some two-thirds of total outstanding bonds. Issuance was particularly strong in the mid- to late-1980s when a boom occurred in Swedish real estate. These bonds, which are mostly in "bullet" form with maturities of two or five years are used to fund the mortgage institution's portfolio, thereby avoiding maturity mismatches. The main purchasers are institutional investors in Sweden, such as the National Pension Fund and insurance companies, and foreign investors. Mortgage bonds are sold continuously on tap, with a number of banks and securities firms acting as issuing houses and market makers. At the same time, other securities such as notes and certificates have been used for shorter-term borrowing. Some of the mortgage institutions have also launched bonds in foreign currencies and euro-commercial paper programmes.

Through the early 1980s the market was highly controlled, with banks, insurance companies and the National Pension Fund obliged to purchase government and mortgage bonds at sub-market interest rates and with cross-border investment (both inward and outward) prohibited. Beginning in the mid-1980s, however, controls were loosened and the Swedish fixed-income market took on the properties of a well-developed, liquid securities market with close linkages to the international capital markets. Trading volume in government bonds is much higher than in mortgage bonds, but the latter are liquid as well. An active market in derivatives also emerged.

Swedish mortgage bonds are unsecured, *i.e.* the investor has no claim against particular assets but a generalised claim against the issuing institution, and therefore the credit standing of the institution is critical. The mortgage institutions are generally required to maintain an 8 per cent capital/assets ratio. In recent years the Swedish real estate market has plunged and delinquencies have risen. Loan-to-value ratios have deteriorated. Although the deterioration in credit quality of the mortgage institutions has not been comparable to that of banks and most mortgage institutions are judged to be financially sound, investors have become more wary and borrowing costs have been increasing. Before 1990, the spread of mortgage bonds over government bonds was fairly tight, but as problems with real estate mounted spreads became very wide in 1990. Despite some subsequent narrowing, spreads remain noticeably higher than before 1990.

The traditional system of mortgage finance has come under pressure from other sources as well. With the end of restrictions on institutions in 1985 and 1986 and the liberalisation of exchange controls in 1989, mortgage bonds could no longer be placed through traditional privileged channels. Additionally, Swedish regulations for insurance companies, which have been changed to conform to EC norms, will limit exposures to individual borrowers. For the largest mortgage institutions, this may require some restructuring of their portfolios. Increasingly, in recent years use has been made of international capital markets. At the same time, given the decline in the value of part of the underlying collateral, direct sale of mortgage bonds to international investors may have to be made at higher costs. In this context, securitisation would be one way of lowering funding costs.

To date, a number of securitisation transactions have involved the international placement of mortgage-backed securities using Swedish mortgages as collateral. A major series of operations was undertaken by SE-Banken, at the time the country's largest commercial bank, to securitise mortgages originated by Svensk Fastighetskredit (SFK), a wholly-owned mortgage subsidiary of SE-Banken; SFK remains the servicer. These operations were known as ''Osprey'' operations, since the issuer of the securities was Osprey Mortgage Securities Ltd., a subsidiary of Jersey-based Osprey Mortgage Securities Holding Ltd. (See table.) After studying possible means of developing a legally sound structure, it was decided to create an SPV based in Jersey. The receivables consisted of fixed-rate mortgages in Swedish currency from the SFK portfolio. The assets were swapped into floating rate dollars. Credit enhancement took the form of pool insurance from Trygg-Hansa Insurance Ltd., and SE-Banken provided a liquidity facility. The first security which resulted from these operations was a five-year US dollar-denominated FRN listed on the Luxembourg Stock Exchange and rated AAA. Following the initial offering, seven more ''Osprey'' operations were launched through 1993 with three in dollars and four in Swedish currency. Total issues through half-year 1994 amounted to over US$1.3 billion.

Swedish mortgage-backed securities

Programme	Issued	Size	Arranger
Osprey 1	1990	$160 million	CSFB
Osprey 2-6	1990	SKr 2.5 billion	Nomura
Osprey 7	1992	£387 million	Goldman Sachs
Osprey 8	1993	$73 million	Goldman Sachs
Fulman	1994	$332 million	Morgan Stanley

Source: IFR. International Securitisation Report, various issues.

With these operations launched successfully, the use of off-balance-sheet securitisation could become more widespread. In addition, preparations are under way to modify domestic legal and regulatory structures so as to facilitate the issue of mortgage-backed securities in the domestic market, rather than through the continued use of offshore facilities.

Several private banks, as well as the authorities, have undertaken surveys to determine whether any serious barriers to wider securitisation of mortgages exist in Sweden. Most of the problems identified would appear to be minor. In the first place, since the concept of a trust is not found in Swedish law, the creation of an offshore SPV was required for the Osprey deals; if the authorities seek to promote widespread securitisation, changes in domestic laws would probably be preferable to permit easier creation of asset-backed or mortgage-backed securities in the domestic market. Swedish accounting and regulatory practices would not appear to present any undue obstacles. One additional problem is that it is not yet clear whether the present capital adequacy rules should apply to SPVs.

The difficulties in the mortgage finance sector have appeared at the same time that other financial institutions have experienced difficulties, often related to real estate. In particular, the commercial banks before 1990 had ratios that exceeded BIS standards by a considerable margin. However, in the past three years, loan losses and non-performing assets have mounted, requiring widespread government intervention. The government has purchased large equity stakes in two banks, extended special loans at concessional rates and issued government guarantees to ensure the survival of two other banks. In two cases, Nordbanken and Gota Bank, the bad loan portfolios were removed and placed in institutions (Securum for Nordbanken and Retriva for Gota Bank) specialising in impaired asset workouts. In December 1993, it was announced that Nordbanken and Gota Bank (both acquired by the Swedish Government as a result of the banking crisis) would be merged to form a new bank which would be the largest commercial bank in the country. It is planned to privatise this bank in the near future.

In view of the need to shrink balance sheets of banks, there has been a growing interest among financial institutions as well as the Swedish authorities to consider the broader application of securitisation. To the degree that asset securitisation can be used to reduce the size of balance sheets of financial institutions, the need for injections of official funds to re-capitalise financial institutions can be lessened. In pursuing related operations in the future, in some circumstances the issuance of mortgage-backed and asset-backed securities using internationally tested techniques may be an additional means of restructuring the financial sector in Sweden. The limited current capacity of the banking system to lend may be a rather minor consideration at this time, but it could become more important once the demand for credit revives.

In addition to developing alternative funding techniques for financial institutions, securitisation could be used in dealing with the overhang of impaired assets in Sweden. A number of banks have sizeable impaired asset portfolios, particularly related to commercial real estate, and the portfolios of Securum and Retriva consist almost exclusively of impaired assets. The use of securitisation techniques, especially those for disposing of impaired assets, might be one way of removing impaired assets from the balance sheets of credit institutions while encouraging high rates of recovery. The experience of the RTC in comparable circumstances may be relevant.

In conclusion, if conditions are created for securitisation in the Swedish credit market, the result could be more effective resource allocation and lower borrowing costs. These benefits can be obtained because credit institutions will have access to better risk management techniques and will be able to differentiate (and thereby lower) their funding costs. Thus, financing could be obtained in accord with market conditions from resident as well as non-resident investors.

Switzerland

The Swiss mortgage market has long been financed in part by the issue of mortgage bonds, *i.e.* in a manner comparable to securitisation. Any Swiss bank, providing it belongs to a "Central Mortgage Institution", is authorised to finance its mortgage lending through the mortgage bond system. Two financial institutions serve as Central Mortgage Institutions: the Mortgage Bond Office of the Swiss cantonal banks and the Swiss mortgage lenders' Mortgage Bond Bank.

The Central Mortgage Institutions are financed through mortgage bond issues which enable them in turn to refinance their member banks' mortgage lending. These refinancing loans must be backed by mortgages that match them exactly, and this method of Swiss bank financing is governed by stringent legislation. An important restriction on the issue of mortgage bonds is that maturities must be long: they are generally issued for twelve years. Moreover, in Switzerland, holders of such bonds (for the most part, institutional and individual Swiss investors) possess preferential junior creditor status. This status, combined with strict legislation (rigorous regulation and supervision of issuing institutions, prudent taxation of bonds, etc.), means that the yields on mortgage bonds are relatively low, with premiums of only half a point over federal government bonds.

The Swiss mortgage market is relatively large, with aggregate loans equal to 130 per cent of the gross national product. The concept of a mortgage bank *per se* is unknown in Switzerland, and any financial institution – especially banks – may engage in mortgage lending. Seventy per cent of Swiss mortgages carry variable interest rates (*i.e.* rates subject to periodic adjustment), and the remainder fixed rates. Theoretically, variable-rate loans may be prepaid with three months' notice. But since, for tax reasons, mortgages are generally not amortised, the principal remains on the lender's balance sheet for long periods of time.

The Swiss market for mortgage bonds represents between 5 and 10 per cent of outstanding mortgages and about 15 per cent of the total domestic bond market. Apart from the Federal Government, the Central Mortgage Institutions are the two most important players in the Swiss bond market. Nonetheless, banks still use the mortgage bond system relatively little, compared to direct financing methods. In particular, savings deposits and commercial paper (with maturities of three to eight years) constitute a less costly and more flexible source of funds than bonds. Most variable-rate mortgages are financed by savings deposits, whereas commercial paper is used to fund fixed-rate loans.

Thanks to that strategy, assets and liabilities are suitably matched and interest rate risk is reduced. Over time, this financing policy has also given Switzerland the world's lowest mortgage rates.

As a result, only in exceptional periods has mortgage securitisation been seen in Switzerland as a good way of satisfactorily matching assets and liabilities. A series of extraordinary, short-lived disturbances in the Swiss bank financing system a few years back led to securitisation being seriously considered. This led to the publication, on 16 September 1991, of a report by a committee of experts commissioned by the Swiss Government to investigate the long-term financing of the mortgage market. The report stressed the need to create a special legal and tax framework so that mortgages could be securitised. Not surprisingly, the report had only a modest impact in Swiss financial circles.

Nevertheless, a first step towards establishing a special framework for securitisation in Switzerland was taken with the 1994 Investment Fund Act. This law broadened the scope of traditional legislation on the subject and now allows the creation of funds that invest in mortgages. Thus securitisation of mortgages would now appear possible in Switzerland, inasmuch as investment funds have been exempt from stamp duty since April 1993. However, it is doubtful – for the reasons mentioned – whether a market for securitised mortgages will develop in Switzerland in the years ahead.

Turkey

The basic legal framework for the securitisation of receivables and fixed assets was established with the amendments to the Capital market Law enacted in 1992 and the related *Communiqué* of the Capital Market Board issued in July 1992.

The *Communiqué* defines asset-backed securities (ABS) as securities issued by general finance corporations, banks, leasing companies and consumer credit companies and backed by the receivables which either stem from their own operations or are bought under the provisions of the *Communiqué* to be registered by the Capital Market Board (CMB). According to the Article 4 of the *Communiqué*, types of receivables that can be subject of the operation are:

- *i)* Banks' and consumer credit companies' consumer loans;
- *ii)* banks' housing loans including mortgage-backed ones;
- *iii)* receivables from the financial leasing agreements;
- *iv)* receivables from exports;
- *v)* joint stock companies and State Economic Enterprises' receivables from instalment sales;
- *vi)* agricultural credits of Ziraat Bankasi;
- *vii)* credits given to tradesmen and craftsmen by Halk Bankasi.

Banks can issue ABS against the loans they have originated themselves, mentioned on item *(i)*, *(ii)* and *(iv)* above directly. Banks can also issue ABS against the receivables they have bought from other corporations.

Consumer credit companies and financial leasing companies can issue ABS backed by the receivables from their own operations, mentioned on items *(i)* and *(iii)* above. In order to issue ABS, it is compulsory for General Finance Corporations, leasing companies and consumer credit institutions to obtain a bank's guarantee.

GFCs can issue ABS against all types of receivables mentioned above through buying them from other corporations. GFCs are joint stock corporations which engage only in issuing of ABS. They cannot engage in any other activity. In order to obtain the permission for establishment of a GFC, it is obligatory for GFC to apply to the CMB. However, as of March 1995, no general finance company or consumer credit institution exists in Turkey. Banks are the major issuer of ABS and heavily involved in all phases of the ABS market.

The first issue of ABS was realised in August 1992. Due to the absence of liquidity and reserve requirements, the ABS practice was rapidly adopted by the banks, as they considered it as a mechanism to collect less costly funds. There was TL 36.5 trillion asset-backed securities outstanding in 1993. However, since April 1994, ABS have been subject to liquidity requirements. As a result of this treatment, ABS has lost the property of being a cheap financing mechanism. Hence, as of December 1994, the total nominal value of ABS outstanding decreased to the level of TL 20 trillion.

.

United Kingdom

The United Kingdom represents the largest market in securitised assets outside the United States, with MBS accounting for some 80 per cent of all securitised assets. However, MBS issuance reached its peak in 1988, and the peak of outstandings occurred in 1989. The pace of issuance accelerated in 1993 from the previous year's very low levels, but still remained well below the volumes of 1988-91 (see Table 1). Thus, securitisation remains of only marginal significance for the financial system as a whole, with neither MBS nor the ABS sector showing great dynamism in the past few years. Inasmuch as the legal and regulatory infrastructure does not present any obvious barrier to the expansion of securitisation, the major explanation for the low level of activity is weak demand on the part of market participants. There has been no programme comparable to that in the United States to provide official guarantees for mortgages. The main potential originators (banks and building societies) have adequate capital. Moreover, as a result of sluggish real economic activity in the past few years, loan growth has been slack and the slump in the property market has made MBS issuance more difficult. Nevertheless, in expectation of some pickup in activity and a change in funding conditions, financial intermediaries continue to undertake a moderate amount of securitisation – including some innovative operations – in order to be able to use the technique more widely if the situation changes.

The British residential mortgage market is huge, with an estimated £355 billion outstanding at the end of 1993. It was an explicit policy of the government in the 1980s to encourage widespread home ownership, and there has been a trend since the 1960s for owner-occupied housing to account for a rising share of the housing stock, although the authorities have never undertaken an official programme to guarantee mortgages such as can be found in the United States and Canada. The main traditional providers of mortgage finance have been the building societies (mutual savings banks), which engage in on-balance-sheet lending and which depend mainly on retail deposits (historically, a low-cost source of funding). In the regulated environment that prevailed through the late 1970s, the building societies supplied nearly all housing finance. With restrictions on bank credit expansion, the building societies faced excess demand for mortgages and set both deposit and lending rates on the basis of a cartel-like arrangement. Building societies which have mutual status have been keen to acquire mortgage books, but have remained reluctant to sell mortgage securities to third parties. Because of the relative health of the sector, there has been no necessity to securitise loans. Those societies that have faced balance-sheet difficulties have been merged with other building societies.

Table 1. **MBS and ABS issues in the United Kingdom by type of asset**

(£ million)

	Residential mortgages (first)	Residential mortgages (second)	Commercial mortgages	Lease receivables	Auto receivables	Swap receivables	Personal loans (unsecured)	Other	Total
1985	50	–	–	–	–	–	–	–	50
1986	–	–	–	–	–	–	–	–	–
1987	1 000	–	–	–	–	–	–	–	1 000
1988	3 301	–	–	–	–	–	–	–	3 301
1989	2 427	–	–	–	–	–	–	–	2 427
1990	2 246	–	–	–	328	–	–	–	2 574
1991	2 759	–	–	–	450	–	–	–	3 209
1992	298	170	–	563	200	–	–	62	1 293
1993	913	92	135	165	294	116	450	100	2 266
1994	2 563	–	333	88	–	–	237	153	3 375
Total	15 558	262	468	816	1 272	116	687	315	19 494

Source: CS First Boston, Barings.

In the mid-1980s, the mortgage and property markets boomed, the volume of outstanding mortgage credit rose very rapidly ,and the financial market was deregulated. The building societies were allowed to compete with banks in offering a number of financial services, while banks were freed from credit restraints. By 1982, banks were doing some 36 per cent of all new residential mortgage lending. At first there was some net decline in savings deposits in the building societies, requiring the latter to borrow on a largescale in the money and capital markets; later in the 1980s as interest rates rose, however, a reflow of retail savings into the building societies occurred. Even in the money and capital markets, the building societies were able to borrow on favourable terms. At the same time, the building societies face regulatory ceilings which limit wholesale funding to 40 per cent of liabilities. Although the commercial banks gained in market share in the 1980s, the building societies still accounted for almost two-thirds of total mortgage lending in 1993. In addition to these institutions which engaged in on-balance-sheet mortgage lending, in 1985-86 specialised mortgage lenders (SMLs) were formed; these rely primarily on off-balance-sheet securitisation as a funding technique. SMLs account for some 6 per cent of mortgage lending (see Table 2).

Table 2.   **MBS and ABS issues in the United Kingdom by type of originator**

(£ million)

	Centralised leaders	Bank	Leasing company	Insurance company	Other	Total
1985	–	50	–	–	–	50
1986	–	–	–	–	–	–
1987	900	100	–	–	–	1 000
1988	2 106	735	–	–	460	3 301
1989	1 777	475	–	175	–	2 427
1990	1 771	803	–	–	–	2 580
1991	2 219	–	450	150	390	3 209
1992	360	370	563	–	–	1 293
1993	463	1 637	165	–	–	2 266
1994	562	2 538	88	–	186	3 375
Total	10 158	6 708	1 266	325	1 036	19 494

Source: CS First Boston, Barings.

Mortgages tend to have maturities of about 25 years at variable rates. Rates are usually reset at six-month intervals. The lender is not obliged to align the lending rate with market rates, but tends to do so, since the borrower has the option to prepay with only a small fee. Recently, there has been a trend toward mortgages that are fixed for relatively long periods. Many mortgages have recently had rates fixed for as long as ten years, but fixed-rate mortgages of up to 25 years are available. Although more than half of new mortgages in 1993 were at fixed rates, the figure for outstanding mortgages was less than 10 per cent. In the past, most mortgages were annuity mortgages in which principal and interest are repaid over the life of the loan with the share of principal rising over time. At this time, only about one-fifth of mortgages are in annuity form. The endowment mortgage now accounts for about four-fifths of the total. Under this system, the borrower takes out an endowment insurance policy at the beginning of the loan, which is assigned to the mortgagee who receives the principal at maturity of the policy or upon the death of the borrower.

As mentioned above, the SMLs specialise in mortgage origination and servicing while relying on securitisation as a funding technique. In an effort to introduce the securitisation techniques developed in the United States, three non-bank-affiliated SMLs were formed, one of which was a subsidiary of Salomon Brothers; several SMLs were also established as subsidiaries of British or foreign banks. Mortgage loans are sold to an SPV which issues securities, most commonly sterling floating rate notes (FRNs). Coupons are typically set quarterly at a stipulated spread over Libor. As in other MBS markets, interest and principal (including prepayments) are passed through to investors. Some innovative MBS issues have been made in the United Kingdom. Similarly, some securities with multiple-tranche sequential pay have been issued, emulating some of the cash flow restructurings that are used in the MBS sector in the United States. By the end of March 1992, total issues by SMLs amounted to £11.2 billion, which represented more than 90 per cent of total MBS issues and 3 per cent of total mortgages outstanding.

In keeping with standard MBS market practice, these securities are given credit enhancements and are rated by rating agencies. Initially, credit enhancements took the form of guarantees from insurance companies or letters of credit from banks. However, as the ratings of banks and insurance companies have been lowered, this method left the securities vulnerable to downgradings as well. Consequently, while two-thirds of all MBS and ABS were still enhanced by insurance companies at the end of 1993, other techniques, especially subordination, were increasingly used for enhancement. Thus far, nearly all MBS have been rated AAA or AA.

The legal and regulatory framework in the United Kingdom does not present a significant barrier to the expansion of securitisation. The authorities have not made it explicit policy to facilitate the advance of securitisation, but have generally made rules enabling the practice to proceed where market demand proved strong enough to support an expansion.

The Securities and Investment Board, which is responsible for the regulation of investment business, has been willing to approve ABS and MBS offerings. The regulation of banks is undertaken by the Bank of England; the Building Societies Commission assumes a similar role for the building societies. In 1989, the Department of the Environment issued voluntary guidelines aimed at protecting borrowers in cases where the loan is transferred, and since that time borrower protection measures have not been an obstacle to securitisation. Both the Bank of England and the Building Society Commission have been willing to accord off-balance-sheet treatment to MBS and ABS, but have required that all risk inherent in underlying assets be removed in order to obtain off-balance-sheet treatment. The greatest uncertainty concerning regulatory questions in the recent past has involved the risk weighting assigned to MBS. For a time in 1991-92, the authorities ruled that, in line with the capital adequacy guidelines of the Commission of the European Communities, MBS carried on-balance-sheets by banks and building societies would command a 100 per cent capital charge rather than the previously required 50 per cent. Subsequently, however, the 50 per cent risk weighting was restored.

Although the MBS market in the United Kingdom is the largest market in securitised assets outside the United States, it has not expanded as rapidly as predicted by some observers in the late 1980s. Following a sharp rise in new issues that accompanied the establishment of SMLs in 1985-86, outstandings reached a peak of about £3.5 billion in 1988 and have levelled off in subsequent years. The lack of further expansion can be attributed mostly to lack of demand, on the part both of issuers and investors. From the issuer side, the great majority of MBS issues were made by SMLs. The banks used off-balance-sheet securitisation to a very limited degree, and only once has a building society made an issue, a privately placed deal in 1994. Until now, the banks and the building societies, which are adequately capitalised and usually had access to cheap sources of funding, have not had strong incentives to securitise. Consequently, only about 3 per cent of total mortgages in the United Kingdom were securitised. Concerning investors, nearly half of UK-originated MBS are purchased by banks and, to a lesser degree, building societies. A number have also been placed with foreign banks. Since many pension funds are seeking longer-term fixed-rate assets to match their pension liabilities, floating rate instruments do not find a ready reception among these investors. Purchases by insurance companies have been modest.

The emergence of the MBS market in the United Kingdom coincided with a down-turn in the housing market which in turn followed a sharp rise in housing prices in the 1980s. House prices fell by more than 10 per cent nationwide, while in some areas where prices had previously risen sharply – especially the Greater London area and the South-East, the decline reached 30 per cent or more. The decline in the property market has harmed the MBS market in several ways. The rate of mortgage origination has declined considerably. The decline in the value of collateral has required further credit enhancement, making securitisation increasingly expensive. The downgradings of banks and insurance companies triggered downgradings of MBS for which they had offered third-party guarantees. Thus, whereas 93 per cent of ABS and MBS issued by UK residents were originally rated AAA, by February 1994 46 per cent of issues were rated AA. There were also some special problems in the SML sector. The competitive lending rates on building society and bank mortgage operations (due to cheap retail funding) meant that SMLs tended to operate at the risky fringe of the market on high loan-to-value ratios and high income multiples. Consequently, the fall in house prices and the rise in unemployment hit the SMLs disproportionately. The SMLs were also disproportionately exposed to the housing market in the South-East. Having withdrawn from the market for two to three years, some SMLs have recently resumed oroginations. Some MBS were issued with AA rather than AAA rating. Another factor discouraging activity is that a major SML has experienced well-publicised financial difficulties which led to higher-risk premiums on MBS, while the other SMLs have also fallen on hard times due to the contraction in business. Taken together, these developments have led some market participants to look upon the MBS market as risk-prone. Many institutions would no longer purchase subordinated tranches. All of these factors have increased the cost of securitisation, which had never attained a clear cost advantage over more traditional funding techniques. A number of institutions which had been active in the market in the mid- to late 1980s have now withdrawn.

While the MBS market has been in the doldrums for the past few years, many UK institutions believe that there is some potential for expansion, assuming that the property market shows greater buoyancy and that overall loan demand recovers. In addition, there is some increase in the amount of fixed-rate mortgages; and if this trend persists, originators may wish to use securitisation in order to avoid maturity mismatches. Moreover, the building societies face regulatory limits on the use of wholesale funding. In recent times, retail deposits have become a relatively expensive means of financing in relation to both wholesale funding and securitisation. If securitisation were to maintain a clear cost advantage at a time of rising demand for mortgages, the building societies would probably securitise on a significant scale. In 1993, some of the major commercial banks launched MBS issues, while even some of the building societies indicated that they might experiment with securitisation if the retail deposit base contracts and/or if overall mortgage demand firms.

The ABS market is considerably less developed than the MBS market. In 1990, the first ABS issues, using automobile loans as collateral, were brought to market. A number of offerings, backed by automobile loans or consumer credits, were made in the next few years. Through the end of 1992, there were seven term asset-backed security issues with estimated total outstandings of £1.3 billion. In 1993-94, the volume of issues picked up slightly. Thus, ABS issuance in 1993 is estimated to have amounted to £1.3 billion. Many financial institutions believe that it is important to maintain some capacity to operate in the MBS and ABS markets. Thus, a number of ABS issues have been made using an increasingly wide variety of collateral. Some major commercial banks have originated FRNs supported by automobile receivables, leases, nursing home loans, trade receivables, home equity loans and personal loans. In addition, National Home Loans issued a security backed by non-performing mortgages.

In 1994, the flow on new deals continued at a sustained but modest pace. Some automobile companies, or their finance subsidiaries, are planning to launch asset-backed FRNs. Moreover, a number of European (including British) banks are developing multi-seller asset-backed commercial paper programmes in London. In brief, while it still remains to be seen whether demand for securitised assets will increase, the major institutions operating in London continue to develop new deals in order to be well-positioned to participate if the economy and the financial markets develop so as to encourage further securitisation.

United States

Over the past two decades, securitisation has emerged as a distinctive feature of the financial system in the United States. Several factors have encouraged the growth of securitisation. The historic separation between banking and securities business has meant that there are alternative channels for financial intermediation; this system can be contrasted with other systems in which the banks dominate most aspects of financial intermediation, even when financial innovations are introduced. Different classes of institutions (banks, thrift institutions, securities houses, institutional investors) often compete among themselves in devising new products. Within this system, institutions in the investment sector have had an unusually high degree of freedom, by international comparison, to develop and to introduce innovative products. The process of bank disintermediation (*i.e.* replacement of on-balance sheet financing by depository institutions with financing off-balance-sheet financing in securities markets), visible throughout the OECD area has probably progressed farther in the United States than in any other country. One particularly noticeable shift in intermediation has been in mortgage finance. Specifically, over the past two decades, on-balance-sheet financing by the thrift industry has been losing importance in housing finance while that of the capital market has gained. This can be clearly seen in Table 1 which shows the long-term evolution of residential mortgage finance in the United States. As the thrift industry contracted, the emergence of strong demand from institutional investors provided an important alternative channel for housing finance. At the same time, the role of commercial banks has increased somewhat, especially in commercial mortgages.

Many trends in the banking and thrift industries encouraged securitisation. The large outstanding volume of consumer debt at high interest rates has meant that there has been a plentiful supply of the category of assets easiest to securitise. The tradition of fixed-rate mortgages and the resulting risk of large asset/liability mismatches encouraged banks and thrifts to use securitisation. The incentive to securitise became particularly powerful when interest-rate volatility increased after 1970. More recently, with growing emphasis in the banking industry on the efficient use of capital and the control of risk, many US banks are seeking to de-emphasize lending as a source of revenue and instead wish to focus on services that generate fee income. Similarly, depository institutions can generate increased earnings from any given level of capital through securitisation. At various times in the past two decades, US banks, under pressure from regulators, shareholders or rating agencies to improve capital/asset ratios, have considered asset sales to be a cost-efficient way of achieving this objective.

Table 1. **Mortgage debt outstanding**

US$ billion at end of period

	1980	1981	1982	1983	1984	1985	1986	1987	1988	1989	1990	1991	1992	1993	1994
All-holders	1 460.4	1 566.7	1 641.1	1 828.8	2 054.6	2 312.8	2 615.4	2 963.2	3 248.6	3 549.6	3 761.6	3 923.4	4 042.6	4 218.7	4 409.4
1 to 4-family	965.1	1 039.8	1 081.7	1 199.4	1 335.1	1 504.7	1 707.1	1 936.1	2 169.3	2 408.4	2 615.4	2 778.4	2 953.8	3 146.4	3 339.2
Multifamily	142.3	142.1	145.8	160.9	185.7	215.6	251.8	276.0	293.7	306.5	309.4	306.4	295.0	292.1	292.2
Commercial	255.5	277.5	302.2	354.8	421.4	486.6	561.3	663.4	702.7	754.2	758.3	759.0	713.7	699.5	695.5
Farm	97.5	107.2	111.3	113.7	112.4	105.9	95.2	87.7	83.0	80.5	78.4	79.1	80.4	80.8	82.5
							Breakdown in percentage								
I. Residential[1]	100.0	100.0	100.0	100.0	100.0	100.0	100.0	100.0	100.0	100.0	100.0	100.0	100.0	100.0	100.0
Commercial banks	16.6	16.4	16.1	15.2	14.7	14.2	13.8	14.2	15.4	16.2	17.4	17.4	17.2	17.7	18.3
Savings institutions	50.5	48.2	42.3	40.2	39.6	36.8	32.7	31.1	31.0	27.8	22.9	19.4	16.6	15.0	14.2
Life insurance companies	1.9	1.7	1.5	1.3	1.1	0.8	0.8	0.7	0.5	0.5	0.5	0.4	0.4	0.3	0.3
Federal agencies	6.4	6.5	7.2	7.3	7.3	7.3	7.3	6.2	5.8	5.5	5.9	5.9	6.5	7.4	7.5
Pools and trusts[2]	12.6	13.6	17.8	21.6	22.7	25.4	30.4	33.8	33.4	35.0	37.9	40.7	42.3	42.1	42.7
Private mortgage conduits	0.4	0.5	0.7	1.0	1.4	1.6	1.0	1.4	1.6	1.8	2.0	3.0	4.5	5.2	5.5
Individuals and others	11.7	13.1	14.3	13.5	13.2	13.8	13.9	12.6	12.3	13.2	13.3	13.2	12.6	12.2	11.5
II. Commercial	100.0	100.0	100.0	100.0	100.0	100.0	100.0	100.0	100.0	100.0	100.0	100.0	100.0	100.0	100.0
Commercial banks	31.6	32.6	33.9	33.9	36.3	37.2	39.7	40.6	41.3	42.7	44.1	44.4	46.1	46.4	47.9
Savings institutions	24.1	22.9	22.0	23.5	24.9	23.8	21.6	22.8	20.1	17.8	14.4	11.4	9.6	8.9	7.8
Life insurance companies	31.6	31.8	31.0	29.3	26.4	26.2	26.6	25.1	26.7	27.2	28.4	28.2	27.8	26.8	24.6
Pools and trusts[2]	2.1	2.2	2.3	2.1	1.8	1.7	0.0	0.0	0.0	0.0	0.0	0.0	0.0	0.0	0.0
Private mortgage conduits	0.0	0.0	0.0	0.0	0.0	0.0	0.0	0.1	0.3	0.6	0.7	0.9	2.1	3.6	5.3
Individuals and others	10.6	10.5	10.8	11.3	10.6	11.1	12.1	11.4	11.6	11.7	12.4	15.1	14.5	14.2	13.2

1. 1-4 Family.
2. Federal agency MBS.
Source: Federal Reserve Board.

A marked institutionalisation of wealth has been occurring in the United States, with funds accumulating in the the hands of institutional money managers such as mutual funds, insurance companies, investment managers and pension funds. This large and diverse community of institutional investors had a rising demand for securities with different liquidity, risk and maturity characteristics. In response to this growing demand by investors for assets with attractive risk/return characteristics, investment banks have sought to create instruments specifically tailored to the requirements of particular investors. This has encouraged intermediaries to structure securities with risk tranches differentiated by credit risk, liquidity and maturity that closely match investor preferences. Furthermore, since US institutional investors are accustomed to doing intensive risk analysis, they have not been intimidated by the complexity of some of the structures involved.

Support from and the innovation of Federal agencies were very important, especially in the early development of the market for MBS. With the large number of geographically dispersed banks, official support eased flows of resources among regions and reduced geographic risk concentration at financial institutions. With a large number of originating institutions and disparate systems of documentation at the outset, the securitisation process itself encouraged standardization in underwriting practices, loan documentation and related procedures, as well as an upgrading of systems to monitor payments. Standardisation occurred not because the official regulators imposed such conditions but because orginators sought to make mortgages conform to the standards set by the securitisation agencies in order to improve liquidity. The extension of direct and indirect Federal support (to the securities issued by the agencies) reduced uncertainties while agencies were developing a range of benchmark securities and while the market was developing pricing models for such securities.

The oldest, and still by far the largest, category of securitisation-related assets consists of mortgage-backed securities, the great majority of which are issued and guaranteed by a government-sponsored enterprise. The outstanding volume of these securities exceeds $1.3 trillion, making this the second largest category of bonds in the United States after Treasury bonds. These securities fall into the broad category of "government agency paper" – a category of assets fairly close to Treasury securities in terms of credit risk, but with somewhat higher yields.

The process of securitisation began in the early 1970s when the Government National Mortgage Association (GNMA) and the Federal Home Loan Mortgage Corporation (FHLMC), agencies of the Federal Government, commenced programmes to securitise residential mortgages originated by banks, thrifts or mortgage companies. A third federal agency, the Federal National Mortgage Association (FNMA) also began securitising mortgages in the early 1980s. In the cases of banks and thrifts, institutions which hold mortgages-on-balance sheet, the securitised assets are removed from the balance sheet. Federal agencies also securitise mortgages originated by mortgage companies, institutions which engage exclusively in off-balance sheet mortgage securitisation, and which now account for a considerable share of the total mortgage market. The legal status and the operating techniques of the three main Federal agencies involved in housing finance are somewhat different. The GNMA, which is an agency within the Federal Government, does not buy loans directly but swaps securities for loans from the originator, and guarantees the resulting pass-through security for an annual fee of 6 basis points. The GNMA will securitise only mortgages insured by the Federal Housing Administration or guaranteed by the Veterans Administration. GNMA recently received legislative authorisation to issue its own CMOs (see below), began doing so in 1994.

The other two agencies, FNMA and FHLMC, which have only indirect ties to the Federal Government, purchase loans for their portfolio directly from lenders. FNMA funds itself partly with direct corporate bonds. FHLMC funds itself partly with direct corporate bonds and also partly by issuing pass-throughs. In addition to purchasing loans, both agencies swap MBS for loans; the swapping lender funds the loans by selling the MBS and pays the agencies a guarantee fee of 20-25 basis points. Both FNMA and FHLMC purchase or securitise primarily "conventional" loans, *i.e.* loans without Federal Housing Administration insurance or Veterans Administration guarantees.

Mortgages securitised by any of these agencies must meet strict credit quality standards and cannot exceed specified amounts. The mortgages are assembled into a "pool" which produces an identifiable cash flow as the backing for marketable "pass through" securities having various maturities and coupon rates. Usually, the originating institution continues as "servicer" of the underlying loans. More than half of the residential mortgages in the United States are now securitised.

Because these securities reflect (or pass through) the cash flows from mortgages, cash flows are significantly different from those on Treasuries, although the credit risk is considered similar. In the normal course of events, principal as well as interest payments will be repaid over the life of the loan, with principal repayments accelerating over time. At the same time, since United States mortgages usually allow borrowers to prepay, there is considerable risk of prepayment for investors. Specifically, in times of falling interest rates, borrowers will tend to prepay mortgages in order to refinance on better terms; at those times investors tend to find that amortisation payments exceed projected amounts, obliging investors to reinvest prepaid principal at lower rates. In essence, investors are able to obtain higher yields on MBS than on Treasury bonds with credit risk that is considered equivalent, but investors must accept greater uncertainty concerning the time profile of repayments.

A major innovation in mortgage-backed financing was the development of collateralised mortgage obligations (CMOs), first introduced in the early 1980s, an instrument which allowed market participants to obtain better control over cash flows from US agency mortgage-backed pass-throughs. This innovation was initially developed by the investment banking community, which began issuing CMOs through dealer conduits using FHLMC pass-throughs as collateral. In 1987, FNMA and FHLMC were authorised to originate CMOs directly, and most agency CMOs are now originated by FNMA or FHLMC, using the "shelf registration" of FNMA or FHLMC rather than that of the investment banks. At the same time, participation by the investment banks in the MBS market is still extensive. The investment banks structure, underwrite and sell the bonds to investors and also deal actively in the secondary market. Dealing activity enables the investment banks to earn significant revenue from trading and also to earn the economic arbitrage between the MBS collateral (which tends to be priced relative to ten-year Treasury bonds) and the CMOs (which are often priced relative to shorter-term Treasuries). The Federal agencies garner fee income from guarantees. By generating greater demand for MBS throughout the investment community, spreads on MBS have tended to narrow. Thus, originators receive better returns than are obtainable through outright sales of mortgages, and the final cost of mortgage finance to borrowers is lowered.

As noted above, one of the difficulties with ''pass-throughs'' is the prepayment risk. CMOs help investors to manage this risk by splitting payments into tranches. In the earlier days of the CMO market, it was common to use a sequential pay structure. Under this mechanism, cash flows were split into four sequential pay (A,B,C and Z) tranches. All payments of principal (including prepayments) are initially directed to the A tranche and successively to B and C tranches. The Z tranche (also known as an accretion bond or accrual bond) will not receive any payment of principal until all principal on earlier tranches is repaid. The A tranche would often have an expected average life of one to three years while the Z tranche would have an expected average life of 15-25 years. Given the highly diversified group of investors in the United States, the varying repayment profiles allow a wider variety of institutions to take different positions among the tranches. Thus, the earlier tranches are often purchased by commercial banks, corporate treasurers or mutual funds while the later tranches are taken up by insurance companies, pension funds and bank trust departments.

In order to attain even further control over cash flows, many CMOs no longer use the simple sequential pay structure described above, but instead use the Planned Amortisation Class (PAC) structure. PAC bonds guarantee investors specific cash flow schedules as long as actual prepayment rates remain within a specified range or band. To guarantee such cash flows, however, PAC bonds are accompanied by ''companion bonds'' or ''support bonds''. These are special tranches that receive residual principal repayments which enable investors in the PAC pay tranches to have greater assurance that actual payments will conform to the initially expected repayment pattern. So long as deviation of actual prepayments from expected prepayments remains within the specified range, the payments of principal are guaranteed to holders of the PAC pay tranches. Meanwhile, the companion bonds absorb all deviations. Due to the fact that they do absorb all unexpected prepayments, companion bonds exhibit high volatility and are priced accordingly.

The creation of multiple class securities (i.e. securities where investors are separated into various categories with regard to the distribution of payments and/or the distribution of risk) created accounting and tax problems. In order to escape double taxation, issuers were obliged to retain some residual interest in the collateral; however, this meant that it was impossible to remove the assets from the balance sheets. The Tax Reform Act of 1986 allowed CMOs and pass-throughs to be issued in the form of Real Estate Mortgage Investment Conduits, (REMICs) by meeting certain requirements. REMICs were eligible for favourable tax and accounting treatment and are now popular with institutional investors. Currently, most CMOs are issued in REMIC form. Moreover, the vast majority of pass-throughs are now transformed, using the CMO mechanism or the REMIC mechanism.

CMOs which are collaterised by agency pass-through, securities or which are rated AAA trade at a spread to comparable Treasury securities reflecting lesser liquidity and the ''prepayment risk.'' With a large volume of assets with low credit risk that is easily tradeable in a diverse investor community, the investment banks have created CMOs based upon agency pass-throughs in which payments on the original tranches can be rearranged in increasingly complex ways so as to meet the specific cash flow requirements of investors. ''Interest only'' and ''principal only'' tranches can be created. Additionally, other transformations can be made, such as converting monthly receipts into quarterly payments. During the period in which the CMO structure is being designed, investment bankers consult widely with the issuing Federal agency and the investor community to transform the aggregate cash flows into specific tranches that match the desired cash flow profiles of investors. In the early 1990s the number and complexity of tranches increased sharply, with some offerings having upwards of 100 tranches. The trend towards more complex structures continued through 1993. After February 1994, however, with interest rates rising and bond markets generally becoming more turbulent, the complex tranches of CMOs became less liquid. In fact, some tranches suffered significant losses of value. Furthermore, rising interest rates have led to a lower rate of refinancing, leading to a decline in MBS origination. Overall, the MBS market since 1994 has been characterised by a smaller volume of new issues and a return to simpler structures.

The market for short-maturity CMO tranches has become very liquid, particularly among money market participants such as banks. Indeed, an OTC derivative market in synthetic CMO tranches has appeared, in which investment banks create synthetic CMOs using swaps which replicate the risk/return characteristics of CMOs but which have some advantages in terms of liquidity and lower administrative costs. The existence of the derivative market has tended to add to liquidity in the short-maturity tranches of CMOs, which in turn adds liquidity to the entire CMO market.

While the CMO or REMIC mechanism can reallocate the prepayment risk of future cash flows to different classes of CMO bonds, the total prepayment risk remains the same. Each security is sold with an expected average life, based upon contractual principal payments and forecast prepayments. Nevertheless, since market conditions nearly always deviate from expected conditions, it is unlikely that the pattern of payments will unfold exactly as expected at the time of the issue of the security. Private financial institutions active in the markets have developed proprietary models to forecast payments on CMOs or REMICs and to price securities accordingly. Prepayment models mainly define payments as a function of the interest rate, time of origination of the underlying collateral (seasoning), housing prices, and the geographic location of the mortgages in the pool. Pricing models recognise that MBS have embedded options for the borrower in which repayments may deviate from the expected pattern in response to variables such as interest rates. Thus, prepayments are likely to accelerate in a falling interest rate environment (call risk), and repayment will be slower than expected in a rising rate environment (extension risk). The models estimate ''fair value'' for mortgage-backed securities, which can be compared to market price.

Thus far, the discussion has only covered mortgage-backed securities which carry government guarantees or which are perceived by the market to have strong government support – hence, the question of credit risk was not important. Eventually, however, a large number of CMOs were issued without official support. (CMOs or REMICs without the support of a Federal agency are termed ''private label''. A certain number of mortgages (known as "non-conforming mortgages") cannot meet the criteria for inclusion in Federal guarantee programmes. Issuers of these securities include home-builders, thrift institutions, banks and mortgage companies.

When mortgage-backed securities began to be issued without strong Federal support in 1977, the problem of analysis and management of credit risk became serious. It is worth remembering that the purchaser of a mortgage-backed security has very limited (and possibly no) recourse to the originator and hence it is important to be sure that: *i)* the receivables are sufficient to generate the payments stipulated in the security; *ii)* safeguards are provided in case of shortfalls in revenue, and *iii)* the investor has a sufficiently clear legal claim on income from the receivables, with adequate protection in case of delinquency.

In order to measure and manage credit risk, the private-label CMO market in the United States developed two major techniques that have now come to characterise the entire international market in mortgage-backed and asset-backed securities: a greatly enlarged role for the rating agencies; and the use of "credit enhancements". With credit risk a serious consideration in all MBS and ABS that do not carry Federal Government support, the rating agencies must examine each deal in detail to determine whether that the collateral and the structure of the security are adequate to justify a particular credit rating (for a fuller discussion of the role of the rating agencies see Section IIB). Concerning the rating agencies, it is now generally expected that all MBS or ABS will carry ratings from at least two agencies.

Over the long term, changes in the relative importance of various forms of credit enhancement can be observed. In general, with the downgrading of many banks and insurance companies, third-party guarantees have declined in importance, although the "monoline" insurers have all retained their high credit ratings and remain a significant force in the market. Overall, senior/subordinated structure over-collateralisation or reserve funds are becoming the most widely used forms of enhancement. The exception is the asset-backed commercial paper market where third-party guarantees and over-collateralisation still constitute the most frequently used forms of enhancement.

The great bulk of securitised assets are still MBS. Nevertheless, since the early 1980s, American financial institutions have been experimenting with the securitisation of other collateral, *i.e.* in developing asset-backed securities. Having developed a set of appropriate mechanisms in the mortgage-backed market, it was a logical step to apply those techniques to create securities backed by other assets. Assets that are most easily securitised are those that involve a large number of homogeneous claims for which the probable rates of delinquency can be estimated based upon historical experience. Furthermore, assets with high margins are best suited to support ABS, since the originator can earn the difference between the rate paid by the investor and the earnings on the underlying collateral. The most commonly used assets are credit card receivables, automobile loans, commercial mortgages (single property and "pools"), leases and home equity loans. Securitisation has progressed farthest in the case of consumer debt. Thus at the end of 1993, an estimated $116 billion in consumer debt (20 per cent of outstanding consumer debt) was securitised. Table 2 presents estimates of all outstanding ABS in the United States since 1983, including asset-backed securities. The outstanding volume of

Table 2. **The asset-backed securities market in the United States**

US$ billion

	1983	1984	1985	1986	1987	1988	1989	1990	1991	1992	1993	1994
Asset-backed securities outstanding												
Collateral												
Consumer credit[a]	–	–	–	–	–	–	48.7	78.5	103.3	121.4	130.7	139.4
Business loans	–	–	–	–	–	–	2.0	5.8	8.8	11.6	21.3	23.3
Trade receivables	0.7	1.5	2.4	3.3	5.1	6.8	8.0	9.2	11.3	13.8	15.2	18.0
Total	0.7	1.5	2.4	3.3	5.1	6.8	60.2	93.7	123.7	155.5	155.6	180.7
of which:												
Asset-backed commercial paper outstanding	0.7	1.5	2.4	3.3	5.1	6.8	15.7	31.4	38.7	47.4	51.9	61.6

a) Mainly automobile loans, consumer loans and credit-card receivables.
Source: Federal Reserve Board.

publicly traded asset-backed securities is estimated at some $160 billion (excluding home equity loans and loans related to housing construction), and annual new issues have averaged $45 billion to $50 billion since 1990.

The capacity of the investment community to construct new instruments based upon new forms of collateral appears limitless. Furthermore, the financial community is seeking at this time to engage in the securitisation of assets, such as commercial real estate loans, commercial loans and small business loans, all of which constitute very large shares of bank lending portfolios but have not yet been securitised on a large scale. Once it becomes possible to securitise such assets on a significant scale, nearly all assets which are currently held in the form of bank credits can be transformed into securities.

There are various hurdles to be overcome if securitisation of certain loan types, especially commercial loans, is to become a reality. First, of course, standardization of underlying loan documents is necessary (as it was for mortgage instruments). This is especially troublesome in commercial lending, where there are almost as many different loan types as there are obligors. Also, credit scoring or grading techniques for individual commercial loans as well as pools of commercial loans are in their infancy. This makes analysing the credit quality of the asset pools backing the securities considerably more difficult for commercial loans than for, say, home mortgages or credit card receivables (where credit grading procedures have been standardied for some time). Finally, there will likely always be a market for ''non-conforming'' assets on the books of banks, as certain borrowers will require (and be willing to pay for) non-standardized treatment.

Asset-backed securities generally have shorter lives than mortgage-backed securities. Indeed, some ABS are issued with money market tranches and sold to money market funds. Despite their relatively short lives, most ABS also contain some prepayment risk.

Asset-backed commercial paper has become a significant part of the US financial market. In fact, the ABS market actually began in the early 1980s with the issue of asset-backed commercial paper (CP). Through 1988, nearly all ABS consisted of asset-backed CP supported by trade receivables. After that time, term ABS were issued and other forms of collateral were used to support asset-backed which now accounts for all net growth in the CP market of the United States since 1986. In the asset-backed CP market, receivables from some commercial activity (most commonly trade receivables, credit card receivables, automobile company receivables or corporate loans) stand as support to a CP facility, a short-term instrument under which borrowers can have direct access to investors for short term funding, usually for no more than 270 days and on average less than 90 days. In these operations, a specified category of receivables is directed into an SPV which may co-mingle receivables from more than one corporate entity or from a single originator, hence the terms ''multi-seller'' or ''single-seller'' facilities. Normally, new receivables enter the facility and other receivables mature continually, so that the asset pool is not fixed.

Although asset-backed CP can be seen as a rather extreme form of bank disintermediation, the banks have played an important part in developing this product. Many banks have viewed this technique as an effective means of earning fees while conserving capital. More than half of all asset-backed CP programmes and about 80 per cent of asset-backed CP outstandings in the United States were bank-advised. Most bank-advised programmes involve the purchase of receivables from a large number of investment grade companies. The credit department of the sponsoring bank analyses the quality of the receivables entering the SPV. Banks also participate in offering credit enhancements, traditionally in the form of letters of credit or liquidity facilities. Recently, as banks' own credit ratings have declined, the markets have required cash collateral from them in lieu of letters of credit. The letter of credit or cash collateral, which constitutes a guarantee against non-payment, may be for a relatively small portion of the amount of the programme, but in some cases may cover the entire programme. On the other hand, liquidity facilities are usually for relatively large amounts but can only be used if the borrower remains creditworthy. Most programmes contain clauses providing for termination of the agreement in case of specific adverse credit developments. Bank facilities to support CP programmes are frequently syndicated among a number of banks. In many instances, banks advise corporate customers to use an asset-backed CP programme rather than a bank loan as the most effective means of funding. Thus, the growth of the asset-backed CP market is both an instance of disintermediation as well as a shift in banks to off-balance-sheet activity as a means of utilising their capital more efficiently.

A number of CP programmes do not directly involve banks as advisors. These programmes usually involve lesser-rated companies and often contain smaller groups of originators (sometimes a single firm, often a retailer). Credit enhancement may take the form of a bank letter of credit or support from a monoline insurer, as well as over-collateralisation, but a bank liquidity facility will normally be used. In many cases, asset-backed CP is an effective funding vehicle for a non-financial company which has a rating of less than investment grade but which has reasonably sound collateral. Asset-backed CP enables the originator to obtain funds on terms more favourable than if the originator were to borrow in its own name. Even some well-rated companies may find this mechanism to be a useful means of diversifying financing.

Another major securitisation-related activity is known as "repackaging" under which a new security is created by purchasing an existing pool of securities, loans or other collateral and restructuring them so as to alter the payments and/or credit rating. In some senses, the simplest "repackaging" operation is similar to the "stripping" of Treasury securities in which an investment bank purchases Treasuries and sells the principal and interest payments to different investors. The CMO mechanism, as described above, always involves considerable "repackaging" of the cash flows of underlying collateral (such as FNMA or FHLMC pass-throughs). Private-label CMOs as well as many ABS operations involve some alteration of the credit risks of collateral. The swap market may be used to transform some of the characteristics of the assets. In addition to changing patterns of cash flow, "repackaging" can alter credit risk through the use of enhancements. Specialised structured instruments known as "collateralised loan obligations" and "collateralised bond obligations" consist of pools of speculative-grade loans or bonds. Cash flows from these assets can be divided into a number of tranches with various degrees of seniority. LDC debt is often "repackaged" in this way; thus investment banks have discovered "excess collateralisation" in some "Brady bonds" and resold the resulting cash flows.

A major expansion in the scope of securitisation has been achieved with the Resolution Trust Corporation (RTC), formed by Congress in 1989 to deal with the problem of insolvent savings and loan institutions (''S&Ls'' or ''thrifts''). The RTC was given the mandate of liquidating the assets of insolvent S&Ls once the primary regulator (the Office of Thrift Supervision) declares the thrift insolvent and appoints the RTC as receiver or conservator. Congress instructed the RTC to sell quickly at favourable prices and to work with private institutions. By June 1993, the RTC had taken control of 737 failed thrifts with total assets exceeding $430 billion, of which some $367 billion had been sold or collected. (In addition to devising new techniques to dispose of assets, there were of course other essential aspects to the work of rehabilitation, such as improving internal audits and upgrading standards of documentation and reporting, but these were performed by other agencies.)

The RTC utilised a variety of techniques in disposing of assets, beginning with ''whole bank sales'' a process in which negotiations were undertaken with solvent institutions to purchase the entire balance sheets (assets and liabilities) of failed institutions at estimated market value. Only a certain amount of assets could be liquidated in this way; thus, in later operations the RTC began to stress the sale of assets, or groups of assets, rather than of whole institutions. Securities – ranging from Treasury paper to junk bonds – accounting for about $125 billion were sold on the market. Many other assets were sold in ''whole loan'' form, *i.e.* without conversion to a security. Most whole loan sales were made to investment banks, but some commercial banks also made significant purchases. Similarly, the RTC began a programme of ''bulk sales'' in which investors were offered pools of assets (usually commercial mortgage loans or real estate) which included some performing loans, sub-performing loans and real estate. In these non-securitised sales, the purchaser was usually an investment bank or an investor who wanted to acquire managerial control over the asset (usually real estate). The RTC found that most of the assets sold by either of these methods were eventually securitised, using ''repackaging'' operations undertaken by the purchasers.

After April 1992, securitisation became the RTC's preferred method for disposing of assets. Some $42 billion in assets have been liquidated through direct securitisation using several techniques. A certain number of assets were relatively easy to securitise. Some mortgages were eligible for inclusion in FNMA or FHLMC pools, but the largest share of single-family mortgage loans did not conform to Federal agency standards. These mortgage loans were sold as RTC private-label single-family pass-throughs or REMICs, and credit-enhanced through a reserve fund and subordination. Investors in the securities are protected so long as the defaults remain within the limits of the reserve funds. The RTC exposure was limited to the amount of the reserve funds. Consumer receivables were also relatively easy to securitise. A number of somewhat more difficult mortgages were eventually securitised in large numbers, including single-family mortgages with high delinquency rates, pools of multi-unit residential mortgages, mobile home loans and commercial mortgages. Senior tranches of most RTC securitisations have been rated AA or AAA. These securitisations used conventional techniques of engaging the services of investment banks as advisers, assembling groups of investment banks, and soliciting competitive bids to lead-manage and distribute issues.

Having successfully begun the process of securitisation, it was necessary to turn to assets that were less easy to sell. In doing so, the RTC encountered problems similar to those that have persistently hampered the securitisation of commercial mortgages. In particular, whereas loan agreements on residential mortgages are rather homogeneous and easy to consolidate into pools, terms on commercial mortgages tend to be very specific, and thus less amenable to consolidation. Moreover, it is difficult to develop statistically credible payment histories to serve as a guide for likely rates of delinquency. The large average size of commercial mortgages makes it harder to achieve acceptable diversification. These difficulties hold for all commercial mortgages but, in the case of the S&Ls, the sharp decline in property values resulted in a large number of non-performing assets and further aggravated the problem. Nevertheless, the RTC has been able to securitise pools of commercial mortgages with credit enhancement. The different tranches of these securities have been rated from AAA (the highest rating) to B (less than investment grade). Some have been done at fixed rates, and others at floating rates. Spreads over Libor ranged from 90 basis points for a AAA offering to 375 basis points for the B tranches.

The RTC had to sell still less liquid assets. There was a large amount of non-performing or ''underperforming'' mortgages which required foreclosure and/or renegotiations of terms. Moreover, some real estate was directly owned by the RTC as a result of foreclosures. RTC officials decided to consolidate these hard-to-sell assets in ''structured transactions''. Like the bulk-sales packages, these operations allow investors to alter the packages of assets but, in general, a mix of attractive and ''problem'' assets must be accepted. The RTC selects a sales agent to market the assets, manage the bidding process and select the investor. The property is sold at a discount to market value and the investor assumes control in return for an asset with significant potential for appreciation, provided that the assets are managed properly. For example, in one transaction in 1992, a pool of 162 non-performing mortgages and 12 non-performing non-investment grade properties were sold to a joint venture of a financial services firm and a real estate investor. The book value was $1 billion, the appraised value $725 million and the cash price $507 million. While the assets were sold at deep discounts, it was deemed imperative to transfer ownership since the property would degrade if not properly maintained.

The senior securities which were rated AA or AAA were widely distributed. Some of the intermediate tranches contained provisions that if the equity partners were unable to begin making full payments by a specified time, interest and/or amortisation would be delayed; usually any delay would mean that the interest rate would be increased. In view of the high levels of security, holders of the intermediate tranches often wish for a slow rate of repayment, while equity holders have a strong incentive to repay as quickly as possible.

In normal circumstances, it is expected that all revenue to service the senior tranches will come from the property, usually through liquidation, rather than from the cash reserves. Thus, on pools of non-performing assets, the revenue can come from *a)* improved servicing or *b)* liquidation. In many cases, a servicer is able to improve the rate of collection simply by improving management of the servicing company. Thus, in failed institutions, key personnel may have left while monitoring and foreclosure procedures may have degraded. In the simplest case, the application of improved monitoring and collection procedures can increase revenue. In other cases, borrowers' capacity to repay may be impaired and it may be necessary to renegotiate terms. Finally, foreclosure proceedings can be initiated against delinquent borrowers and property can be liquidated.

The equity interest tranche was frequently divided in a ''partnership agreement'' between the RTC and a private investor. In early deals, the RTC share of equity ranged from 25-51 per cent, but eventually the RTC generally accepted a 51 per cent share of equity with private investors holding the reminder. In many cases, the equity investors consisted of professional managers of real estate who worked in partnership with cash-rich investors who were willing to accept high risk for high returns. Normally, the cash reserve was meant merely to provide liquidity in the early phases. The revenue for the payment of interest and principal was expected to come from the collateral.

Overall the RTC was able to sell massive amounts of assets, many of which were not easily marketable, in a comparatively short time. There are both positive and negative aspects of the broad use of securitisation as a technique to dispose of assets. On the one hand, the RTC maintains that the prices received through securitisation were more favourable than those received from alternative methods. On the other hand, the ''prices'' received by the RTC for its impaired assets do not reflect the credit enhancements offered by the RTC, so that future losses on the underlying assets may result in further losses to the RTC. Thus, it is not entirely clear that utilising the securitisation route will result in fewer losses to the RTC than would outright sales of assets at distressed prices. At the very least, by selling assets relatively quickly it succeeded in limiting the need for further Federal support. The RTC also retains the cash reserve funds for every performing loan and an equity interest in every non-performing loan securitisation. The value of the reserve funds and the equity interest may increase or decrease over time, depending upon the performance of the securitised assets. The RTC plans to sell its reserve funds and equity interest once the securities develop a payments record (become seasoned). Table 3 summarises RTC securitisation activity. As can be seen, the number of securitisation operations peaked in 1992. In 1993, the new Administration decided that other approaches to disposing of the remaining $100 billion in assets would be tried. As a result, the volume of new issuance contracted sharply in 1993-94.

With an active market in securities based upon impaired assets now established and with the RTC having reduced activity, the pace of issues by private institutions may quicken. Many banks and insurance companies apparently are considering the use of this method to sell their portfolios of impaired real estate. Regulatory or market capital requirements may preclude widespread use of such a technique, however; the securitisation of impaired assets may require that such large credit enhancements be offered by the originator and that, for all practical purposes, the assets do not leave the books of the institution.

As mentioned previously, one of the explanations for the rapid advance of securitisation in the United States has been the hospitable legal and regulatory environment. The process of securitisation has been supported by a series of legislative changes which assisted the emergence of relatively favourable legal, tax, accounting and regulatory infrastructure. Those responsible for these systems have been willing to accept the creation of new kinds of securities and to remove obstacles to their introduction. The basic concept of a trust, which is an established principle of American law, proved to be

Table 3. **RTC Securities issuance by category of collateral**

US$ million

	Single-family mortgages	Multi-family mortgages	Commercial real estate mortgages	Mobile home loans	Home equity loans	Total
1991	7 542	2 692	0	0	0	10 234
1992	12 235	1 780	7 189	616	311	22 131
1993	1 115	0	2 130	0	0	3 245
Total issuance	20 892	4 472	9 319	616	311	35 610
Out-standing as of June 1994	10 675	3 214	6 923	332	135	21 279

Source: Federal Reerve Board.

very adaptable to various forms of securitisation. The courts have rendered decisions that enabled originators to transfer assets and to construct the various structures needed for increasingly complex operations.

The regulatory authorities have generally been supportive by accepting the removal of various assets from bank balance sheets. Mortgage-backed securities received favourable treatment under US applications of international capital adequacy guidelines. Thus, GNMA securities have a zero risk weighting (the same as Treasury bonds), while FNMA and FHLMC securities or private CMOs collateralised with securities from any of these agencies receive a 20 per cent risk weighting. Private mortgage-backed securities without Federal agency paper as collateral carry a 50 per cent risk weighting. At the same time, US banking regulators are known to be thinking intensively about the concept of recourse. One associated issue is that they consider it important that the regulatory burden fall equally on transactions with equal risk. For example, losses normally amount to less than 100 per cent of contractual payments; thus a bank making a loan of a given amount would be required to hold 8 per cent capital, but while a bank offering a letter of credit for 25 per cent of the credit risk under a CP facility would only be required to hold 2 per cent, the risk may actually be very similar. Should the US regulators significantly tighten capital requirements on credit enhancements – including recourse – offered by banks on various securitisations, this may slow down the utilisation of existing structures and/or delay the development of new forms of securitisation.

The Securities and Exchange Commission has made of series of decisions that recognised mortgage-backed and asset-backed securities, and facilitated their issuance. For example, in October 1992, the SEC allowed shelf registration of investment grade asset-backed securities. Expanded access to the shelf registration process permits a broad range of previously ineligible financial assets to be offered and sold on a delayed basis, thereby reducing transactions costs. In November 1992, restrictions on the kinds of collateral that can be used in asset-backed securities were eased, by adopting a conditional exemption (Rule 3a-7) from application of the Investment Company Act of 1940 for investment grade ABS that are supported by a wide range of financial assets.

Bibliography

Books

ADELSON, Mark H. (1993), "Asset-Backed Commercial Paper: Understanding the Risks" in *Structure Finance – Research & Commentary*, Moody's Investors Service, New York.

BANK FOR INTERNATIONAL SETTLEMENTS (1994), *National Differences in Interest Rate Transmission*, Basel.

BISHOP, Graham (1990), *1992 and Beyond: Higher Bank Capitalisation Equals Securitisation*, Salomon Brothers, London.

CARRON, Andrew S. (1991), *Introduction to US Mortgage Securities*, First Boston Corporation, New York.

CARRON, Andrew S. (1992), *Understanding CMOs, REMICs, and Other Mortgage Derivatives*, First Boston Corporation, New York.

EUROPEAN MORTGAGE FEDERATION (1989), *The Valuation of Property in the EC Countries*, Brussels.

EUROPEAN MORTGAGE FEDERATION (1989), *Variability of Interest Rates on Mortgage Loans in the EC*, Brussels.

EUROPEAN MORTGAGE FEDERATION (1990), *The Laws Governing the Issuing of Bonds*, Brussels.

EUROPEAN MORTGAGE FEDERATION (1990), *Mortgage Credit in the European Community*, Brussels.

EUROPEAN MORTGAGE FEDERATION (1992), *The Main Refinancing Instruments*, Brussels.

EUROPEAN MORTGAGE FEDERATION (1992), *The Protection of the Mortgage Borrower in the Countries of the European Community*, Brussels.

EUROPEAN MORTGAGE FEDERATION (1992), *Securitisation of Mortgage Backed Securities in the EC*, Brussels.

EUROPEAN MORTGAGE FEDERATION (1993), *Credit to Public Authorities and Institutions in the EC*, Brussels.

EUROPEAN MORTGAGE FEDERATION (1993), *Mortgage Banks and the Mortgage Bond in Europe*, Nomos Verlagsgesellschaft, Baden-Baden.

FABOZZI, Frank J., ed. (1992), *The Handbook of Mortgage-Backed Securities, Third Edition*, Probus Publishing Company, Chicago.

FERNANDEZ RICO, J.M. (1993), "The Spanish Property Market" in *The Mortgage and Real Estate Market in Spain*, European Mortgage Federation, Brussels.

FINGLETON, M. and D. FLINTER (1993), *The Mortgage and Financial Market in Ireland*, European Mortgage Federation, Brussels.

FIRST BOSTON CORPORATION (1992), *Asset-Backed Securities: Manufactured Housing Loans*, New York.

GAIVO, P. (1991), "The Real Estate Market in Portugal" in *The Mortgage and Real Estate Market in Portugal*, European Mortgage Federation, Brussels.

GOMEZ ABREO, J. (1991), "The Mortgage Market in Portugal" in *The Mortgage and Real Estate Market in Portugal*, European Mortgage Federation, Brussels.

GRANGIER, J.-C. (1993), "The Financing of the Property Market in Switzerland" in *The Mortgage and Real Estate Market in Switzerland* , European Mortgage Federation, Brussels.

GURTNER, P. (1993), "Housing Construction and the Promotion of Home Ownership in Switzerland" in *The Mortgage and Real Estate Market in Switzerland*, European Mortgage Federation, Brussels.

HENDERSON, John and Jonathan P. SCOTT (1988), *Securitization*, Woodhead-Faulkner, London.

HUDSON, Tracy and Greg PARSEGHIAN (1992), *Asset-Backed Securities: Credit Card Receivables*, The First Boston Corporation, New York.

HUDSON, Tracy and Greg PARSEGHIAN (1993), *Asset-Backed Securities: Wholesale Dealer Automobile Loans*, The First Boston Corporation, New York.

MAYAYO, G. (1993), "Regulatory Changes Affecting the Spanish Mortgage Market" in *The Mortgage and Real Estate Market in Spain*, European Mortgage Federation, Brussels.

MORRISSEY, Helena, ed. (1992), *International Securitisation*, IFR Publishing Ltd., London.

PUBLIC SECURITIES ASSOCIATION (1992), *An Investor's Guide to REMICs*, New York.

RESOLUTION TRUST CORPORATION (1993), *Guide to RTC Securities*, Washington, DC.

SPRATLIN, Janet and Paul VIANNA (1986), *An Investor's Guide to CMOs*, Salomon Brothers, New York.

STONE, Charles, Anne ZISSU and Jess LEDERMAN, eds. (1991), *Asset Securitisation: Theory and Practice in Europe*, Euromoney Books, London.

UNITED STATES CONGRESSIONAL BUDGET OFFICE (1993), *Resolving the Thrift Crisis*, Washington, D.C.

WHITE, Laurence J. (1991), *The S&L Debacle*, Oxford University Press, New York.

Articles

ALLINI, Eric J, Peter J. ELMER and Frank RAITER (1995), "Principles of Fixed-Income Securities Auctions, *Journal of Fixed Income*, Vol. 5, Number 1, June.

BOEMIO, Thomas R. and Gerald A. EDWARDS (1989), "Securitisation: A Supervisory Perspective", *Federal Reserve Bulletin*, October.

BOYD, J.H. and M. GERTLER (1994), "Are Banks Dead? Or, Are the Reports Greatly Exaggerated?", Federal Reserve Bank of Minneapolis, Working Paper 531, June.

CANTOR, Richard and Rebecca DEMSETZ (1993), "Securitization, Loan Sales and the Credit Slowdown", *Federal Reserve Bank of New York Quarterly Review*, Vol. 18, No. 2, Summer.

CAOUETTE, John B. (1992), "The Future of Asset Securitization", *The World of Banking*, July-August.

CAPUTO-NASSETTI, Francesco (1992), "The Prospect for Securitisation in Italy", *Journal of International Banking Law*, November.

CARROLL, Michael and Alyssa A. LAPPEN (1994), "Mortgage-Backed Mayhem", *Institutional Investor*, July.

DAVIS, Stephen (1993), "The Securitization Challenge", *Institutional Investor*, December.

DEMSETZ, Rebecca (1993), "Recent Trends in Commercial Bank Loan Sales", *Federal Reserve Bank of New York Quarterly Review*, Winter.

DEUTSCHE BUNDESBANK (1987), "Changes in the Structure of the Public Authorities' Debt Since 1980", *Monthly Report of the Deutsche Bundesbank*, April.

DEUTSCHE BUNDESBANK (1987), "New Off-balance Financial Instruments and Their Implications for Banks in the Federal Republic of Germany", *Monthly Report of the Deutsche Bundesbank*, April.

DEUTSCHE BUNDESBANK (1989), "The Finance of the Local Authorities Since 1988", *Monthly Report of the Deutsche Bundesbank*, November.

DEUTSCHE BUNDESBANK (1989), "Longer-term Trends in the Banking Sector and Market Positions of the Individual Categories of Banks", *Monthly Report of the Deutsche Bundesbank*, April.

DEUTSCHE BUNDESBANK (1992), "The Business of the Mortgage Banks Since the Beginning of the Eighties", *Monthly Report of the Deutsche Bundesbank*, April.

DEUTSCHE BUNDESBANK (1995), "Trends Toward Securitisation in the German Financial System and Their Implications for Monetary Policy", *Monthly Report of the Deutsche Bundesbank*, April.

DIAMOND, Douglas B., Jr. and Michael J. LEA (1992), "Chapter 2: Denmark", *Journal of Housing Research*, Vol. 3, Issue 1.

DOWNS, Anthony (1992), "Securitization is One Answer to Liquidity Problems", *National Real Estate Investor*, August.

EDWARDS, Ben (1994), "Investors in Search of a Market", *Euromoney*, April.

EVERLING, Oliver (1993), "Asset Securitisation in Europa", *Die Bank*, February.

FRANTZ, James B. (1992), "Some Traditional Lenders Coming Back: Mortgage Securitization Gains Momentum", *National Real Estate Investor*, October.

FRENKEL, Alan B. and John D. MONTGOMERY (1991), "Financial Structure: An International Perspective", *Brookings Papers on Economic Activity*, January.

HARVEY, David M.W. (1991), "Securitization Goes International", *The Bankers' Magazine*, May/June.

HOOKER, Wade S., Jr. and William H. HAGENDORN (1992), "United States", *International Financial Law Review*, August.

HU, Joseph (1992), "Housing and the Mortgage Securities Markets: Review, Outlook and Policy Recommendations", *Journal of Real Estate Finance and Economics*, 5: 167-179, Kluwer Academic Publishers.

KANDA, Hideki and Michael T. KAWACHI (1993), "Securitisation in Japan", *Japan Credit Rating Financial Digest*, November.

KAVANAGH, Barbara, Thomas R. BOEMIO and Gerald A. EDWARDS, Jr. (1992), "Asset-Backed Commercial Paper Programs", *Federal Reserve Bulletin*, February.

KAWAMURA, Yusuke (1991), "Securitization of Finance", *Fair Fact Series II: Japan's Financial Markets*, Foundation for Advanced Information and Research (FAIR), Japan.

McALLISTER, Patrick H. and John J. MINGO (1994), "Bank Capital Requirements for Securitised Loan Pools", unpublished discussion paper, Board of Governors of the Federal Reserve System, Washington, DC., December.

MOUILLART, Michel (1992), "Les Banques et les Crédits à l'Habitat", *Les Cahiers du Crédit Mutuel*, No. 85, June-July-August.

PARESH, Mashru and Mark RYS (1992), "What Price Security?", *Balance Sheet*, Vol. 1, No. 1, Spring.

POPPER, Margaret (1994), "The Asset-Backed Culture Clash", *Institutional Investor*, February.

POST, Mitchell A. (1992), "The Evolution of the US Commercial Paper Market Since 1980", *Federal Reserve Bulletin*, December.

ROQUETTE, Andreas J. (1994), "New Developments Relating to the Internationalisation of the Capital Markets: A Comparison of Legislative Reforms in the United States, the European Community and Germany", *University of Pennsylvania Journal of International Business Law XV*, Winter.

ROSSNER, Daniel M. and Yoshika SHIMADA (1992), "Japan", *International Financial Law Review*.

SAHLING, Leonard (1992), "The RTC: Managing the Clean-up of the Thrift Crisis", *Merrill Lynch Real Estate Economics Special Report* , April.

SHENKER, Joseph C. and Anthony J. COLLETTA (1991), "Asset Securitisation: Evolution, Current Issues and New Frontiers", *Texas Law Review*, Vol. 69.

STANDARD & POOR CORPORATION (1993), "Development of Securitization Around the World", *The World of Banking*, May-June.

The Financier (1994), "Securitization", Special Section in "Analyses of Capital and Money Market Transactions", December.

TWINN, Ian C. (1994), "Asset-Backed Securitisation in the United Kingdom", *The Bank of England Quarterly Bulletin*, May.

VAN DER HOEVEN, William (1993), "Securitisation of the Swedish Credit Market", *The Swedish Central Bank Quarterly Review*, Vol. 3.

WEISS, Richard (1989), "L'Irrésistible Développement de la Titrisation", *L'Observateur de l'Immobilier*, No. 16.

WEISS, Richard (1995), "Titrisation: En attente du demarrage", *L'observateuer de l'immobilier*, No. 30, January.

Trade Publications

ARTHUR ANDERSEN & COMPANY (1992), "A Linked Presentation for Non-Recourse Finance: ABS Issues Paper on the Accounting Treatment for Securitisations", November.

BEAR STEARNS (1993), "Spanish Peseta Securitisation", Bear Stearns Financial Analytics and Structures Transactions Group, London, December.

DUFF AND PHELPS CREDIT RATING COMPANY (1994), "Securitisation in Europe", London.

MAIN SALES OUTLETS OF OECD PUBLICATIONS
PRINCIPAUX POINTS DE VENTE DES PUBLICATIONS DE L'OCDE

ARGENTINA – ARGENTINE
Carlos Hirsch S.R.L.
Galería Güemes, Florida 165, 4° Piso
1333 Buenos Aires   Tel. (1) 331.1787 y 331.2391
Telefax: (1) 331.1787

AUSTRALIA – AUSTRALIE
D.A. Information Services
648 Whitehorse Road, P.O.B 163
Mitcham, Victoria 3132   Tel. (03) 873.4411
Telefax: (03) 873.5679

AUSTRIA – AUTRICHE
Gerold & Co.
Graben 31
Wien I   Tel. (0222) 533.50.14
Telefax: (0222) 512.47.31.29

BELGIUM – BELGIQUE
Jean De Lannoy
Avenue du Roi 202 Koningslaan
B-1060 Bruxelles   Tel. (02) 538.51.69/538.08.41
Telefax: (02) 538.08.41

CANADA
Renouf Publishing Company Ltd.
1294 Algoma Road
Ottawa, ON K1B 3W8   Tel. (613) 741.4333
Telefax: (613) 741.5439
Stores:
61 Sparks Street
Ottawa, ON K1P 5R1   Tel. (613) 238.8985
211 Yonge Street
Toronto, ON M5B 1M4   Tel. (416) 363.3171
Telefax: (416)363.59.63

Les Éditions La Liberté Inc.
3020 Chemin Sainte-Foy
Sainte-Foy, PQ G1X 3V6   Tel. (418) 658.3763
Telefax: (418) 658.3763

Federal Publications Inc.
165 University Avenue, Suite 701
Toronto, ON M5H 3B8   Tel. (416) 860.1611
Telefax: (416) 860.1608

Les Publications Fédérales
1185 Université
Montréal, QC H3B 3A7   Tel. (514) 954.1633
Telefax: (514) 954.1635

CHINA – CHINE
China National Publications Import
Export Corporation (CNPIEC)
16 Gongti E. Road, Chaoyang District
P.O. Box 88 or 50
Beijing 100704 PR   Tel. (01) 506.6688
Telefax: (01) 506.3101

CHINESE TAIPEI – TAIPEI CHINOIS
Good Faith Worldwide Int'l. Co. Ltd.
9th Floor, No. 118, Sec. 2
Chung Hsiao E. Road
Taipei   Tel. (02) 391.7396/391.7397
Telefax: (02) 394.9176

CZECH REPUBLIC – RÉPUBLIQUE TCHÈQUE
Artia Pegas Press Ltd.
Narodni Trida 25
POB 825
111 21 Praha 1   Tel. 26.65.68
Telefax: 26.20.81

DENMARK – DANEMARK
Munksgaard Book and Subscription Service
35, Nørre Søgade, P.O. Box 2148
DK-1016 København K   Tel. (33) 12.85.70
Telefax: (33) 12.93.87

EGYPT – ÉGYPTE
Middle East Observer
41 Sherif Street
Cairo   Tel. 392.6919
Telefax: 360-6804

FINLAND – FINLANDE
Akateeminen Kirjakauppa
Keskuskatu 1, P.O. Box 128
00100 Helsinki
Subscription Services/Agence d'abonnements :
P.O. Box 23
00371 Helsinki   Tel. (358 0) 121 4416
Telefax: (358 0) 121.4450

FRANCE
OECD/OCDE
Mail Orders/Commandes par correspondance:
2, rue André-Pascal
75775 Paris Cedex 16   Tel. (33-1) 45.24.82.00
Telefax: (33-1) 49.10.42.76
Telex: 640048 OCDE
Internet: Compte.PUBSINQ @ oecd.org
Orders via Minitel, France only/
Commandes par Minitel, France exclusivement :
36 15 OCDE
OECD Bookshop/Librairie de l'OCDE :
33, rue Octave-Feuillet
75016 Paris   Tel. (33-1) 45.24.81.81
(33-1) 45.24.81.67
Documentation Française
29, quai Voltaire
75007 Paris   Tel. 40.15.70.00
Gibert Jeune (Droit-Économie)
6, place Saint-Michel
75006 Paris   Tel. 43.25.91.19
Librairie du Commerce International
10, avenue d'Iéna
75016 Paris   Tel. 40.73.34.60
Librairie Dunod
Université Paris-Dauphine
Place du Maréchal de Lattre de Tassigny
75016 Paris   Tel. (1) 44.05.40.13
Librairie Lavoisier
11, rue Lavoisier
75008 Paris   Tel. 42.65.39.95
Librairie L.G.D.J. - Montchrestien
20, rue Soufflot
75005 Paris   Tel. 46.33.89.85
Librairie des Sciences Politiques
30, rue Saint-Guillaume
75007 Paris   Tel. 45.48.36.02
P.U.F.
49, boulevard Saint-Michel
75005 Paris   Tel. 43.25.83.40
Librairie de l'Université
12a, rue Nazareth
13100 Aix-en-Provence   Tel. (16) 42.26.18.08
Documentation Française
165, rue Garibaldi
69003 Lyon   Tel. (16) 78.63.32.23
Librairie Decitre
29, place Bellecour
69002 Lyon   Tel. (16) 72.40.54.54
Librairie Sauramps
Le Triangle
34967 Montpellier Cedex 2   Tel. (16) 67.58.85.15
Tekefax: (16) 67.58.27.36

GERMANY – ALLEMAGNE
OECD Publications and Information Centre
August-Bebel-Allee 6
D-53175 Bonn   Tel. (0228) 959.120
Telefax: (0228) 959.12.17

GREECE – GRÈCE
Librairie Kauffmann
Mavrokordatou 9
106 78 Athens   Tel. (01) 32.55.321
Telefax: (01) 32.30.320

HONG-KONG
Swindon Book Co. Ltd.
Astoria Bldg. 3F
34 Ashley Road, Tsimshatsui
Kowloon, Hong Kong   Tel. 2376.2062
Telefax: 2376.0685

HUNGARY – HONGRIE
Euro Info Service
Margitsziget, Európa Ház
1138 Budapest   Tel. (1) 111.62.16
Telefax: (1) 111.60.61

ICELAND – ISLANDE
Mál Mog Menning
Laugavegi 18, Pósthólf 392
121 Reykjavik   Tel. (1) 552.4240
Telefax: (1) 562.3523

INDIA – INDE
Oxford Book and Stationery Co.
Scindia House
New Delhi 110001   Tel. (11) 331.5896/5308
Telefax: (11) 332.5993
17 Park Street
Calcutta 700016   Tel. 240832

INDONESIA – INDONÉSIE
Pdii-Lipi
P.O. Box 4298
Jakarta 12042   Tel. (21) 573.34.67
Telefax: (21) 573.34.67

IRELAND – IRLANDE
Government Supplies Agency
Publications Section
4/5 Harcourt Road
Dublin 2   Tel. 661.31.11
Telefax: 475.27.60

ISRAEL
Praedicta
5 Shatner Street
P.O. Box 34030
Jerusalem 91430   Tel. (2) 52.84.90/1/2
Telefax: (2) 52.84.93
R.O.Y. International
P.O. Box 13056
Tel Aviv 61130   Tel. (3) 546 1423
Telefax: (3) 546 1442
Palestinian Authority/Middle East:
INDEX Information Services
P.O.B. 19502
Jerusalem   Tel. (2) 27.12.19
Telefax: (2) 27.16.34

ITALY – ITALIE
Libreria Commissionaria Sansoni
Via Duca di Calabria 1/1
50125 Firenze   Tel. (055) 64.54.15
Telefax: (055) 64.12.57
Via Bartolini 29
20155 Milano   Tel. (02) 36.50.83
Editrice e Libreria Herder
Piazza Montecitorio 120
00186 Roma   Tel. 679.46.28
Telefax: 678.47.51
Libreria Hoepli
Via Hoepli 5
20121 Milano   Tel. (02) 86.54.46
Telefax: (02) 805.28.86
Libreria Scientifica
Dott. Lucio de Biasio 'Aeiou'
Via Coronelli, 6
20146 Milano   Tel. (02) 48.95.45.52
Telefax: (02) 48.95.45.48

JAPAN – JAPON
OECD Publications and Information Centre
Landic Akasaka Building
2-3-4 Akasaka, Minato-ku
Tokyo 107   Tel. (81.3) 3586.2016
Telefax: (81.3) 3584.7929

KOREA – CORÉE
Kyobo Book Centre Co. Ltd.
P.O. Box 1658, Kwang Hwa Moon
Seoul   Tel. 730.78.91
Telefax: 735.00.30

MALAYSIA – MALAISIE
University of Malaya Bookshop
University of Malaya
P.O. Box 1127, Jalan Pantai Baru
59700 Kuala Lumpur
Malaysia   Tel. 756.5000/756.5425
                             Telefax: 756.3246

MEXICO – MEXIQUE
Revistas y Periodicos Internacionales S.A. de C.V.
Florencia 57 - 1004
Mexico, D.F. 06600   Tel. 207.81.00
                             Telefax: 208.39.79

NETHERLANDS – PAYS-BAS
SDU Uitgeverij Plantijnstraat
Externe Fondsen
Postbus 20014
2500 EA's-Gravenhage   Tel. (070) 37.89.880
Voor bestellingen: Telefax: (070) 34.75.778

**NEW ZEALAND
NOUVELLE-ZÉLANDE**
GPLegislation Services
P.O. Box 12418
Thorndon, Wellington   Tel. (04) 496.5655
                             Telefax: (04) 496.5698

NORWAY – NORVÈGE
Narvesen Info Center – NIC
Bertrand Narvesens vei 2
P.O. Box 6125 Etterstad
0602 Oslo 6   Tel. (022) 57.33.00
                            Telefax: (022) 68.19.01

PAKISTAN
Mirza Book Agency
65 Shahrah Quaid-E-Azam
Lahore 54000   Tel. (42) 353.601
                            Telefax: (42) 231.730

PHILIPPINE – PHILIPPINES
International Book Center
5th Floor, Filipinas Life Bldg.
Ayala Avenue
Metro Manila   Tel. 81.96.76
                            Telex 23312 RHP PH

PORTUGAL
Livraria Portugal
Rua do Carmo 70-74
Apart. 2681
1200 Lisboa   Tel. (01) 347.49.82/5
                            Telefax: (01) 347.02.64

SINGAPORE – SINGAPOUR
Gower Asia Pacific Pte Ltd.
Golden Wheel Building
41, Kallang Pudding Road, No. 04-03
Singapore 1334   Tel. 741.5166
                            Telefax: 742.9356

SPAIN – ESPAGNE
Mundi-Prensa Libros S.A.
Castelló 37, Apartado 1223
Madrid 28001   Tel. (91) 431.33.99
                            Telefax: (91) 575.39.98

Libreria Internacional AEDOS
Consejo de Ciento 391
08009 – Barcelona   Tel. (93) 488.30.09
                            Telefax: (93) 487.76.59

Llibreria de la Generalitat
Palau Moja
Rambla dels Estudis, 118
08002 – Barcelona
               (Subscripcions) Tel. (93) 318.80.12
               (Publicacions) Tel. (93) 302.67.23
                            Telefax: (93) 412.18.54

SRI LANKA
Centre for Policy Research
c/o Colombo Agencies Ltd.
No. 300-304, Galle Road
Colombo 3   Tel. (1) 574240, 573551-2
                    Telefax: (1) 575394, 510711

SWEDEN – SUÈDE
Fritzes Customer Service
S–106 47 Stockholm   Tel. (08) 690.90.90
                            Telefax: (08) 20.50.21

Subscription Agency/Agence d'abonnements :
Wennergren-Williams Info AB
P.O. Box 1305
171 25 Solna   Tel. (08) 705.97.50
                            Telefax: (08) 27.00.71

SWITZERLAND – SUISSE
Maditec S.A. (Books and Periodicals - Livres
et périodiques)
Chemin des Palettes 4
Case postale 266
1020 Renens VD 1   Tel. (021) 635.08.65
                            Telefax: (021) 635.07.80

Librairie Payot S.A.
4, place Pépinet
CP 3212
1002 Lausanne   Tel. (021) 341.33.47
                            Telefax: (021) 341.33.45

Librairie Unilivres
6, rue de Candolle
1205 Genève   Tel. (022) 320.26.23
                            Telefax: (022) 329.73.18

Subscription Agency/Agence d'abonnements :
Dynapresse Marketing S.A.
38 avenue Vibert
1227 Carouge   Tel. (022) 308.07.89
                            Telefax: (022) 308.07.99

See also – Voir aussi :
OECD Publications and Information Centre
August-Bebel-Allee 6
D-53175 Bonn (Germany)   Tel. (0228) 959.120
                            Telefax: (0228) 959.12.17

THAILAND – THAÏLANDE
Suksit Siam Co. Ltd.
113, 115 Fuang Nakhon Rd.
Opp. Wat Rajbopith
Bangkok 10200   Tel. (662) 225.9531/2
                            Telefax: (662) 222.5188

TURKEY – TURQUIE
Kültür Yayinlari Is-Türk Ltd. Sti.
Atatürk Bulvari No. 191/Kat 13
Kavaklidere/Ankara   Tel. 428.11.40 Ext. 2458
Dolmabahce Cad. No. 29
Besiktas/Istanbul   Tel. (312) 260 7188
                            Telex: (312) 418 29 46

UNITED KINGDOM – ROYAUME-UNI
HMSO
Gen. enquiries   Tel. (171) 873 8496
Postal orders only:
P.O. Box 276, London SW8 5DT
Personal Callers HMSO Bookshop
49 High Holborn, London WC1V 6HB
                            Telefax: (171) 873 8416
Branches at: Belfast, Birmingham, Bristol,
Edinburgh, Manchester

UNITED STATES – ÉTATS-UNIS
OECD Publications and Information Center
2001 L Street N.W., Suite 650
Washington, D.C. 20036-4910 Tel. (202) 785.6323
                            Telefax: (202) 785.0350

VENEZUELA
Libreria del Este
Avda F. Miranda 52, Aptdo. 60337
Edificio Galipán
Caracas 106   Tel. 951.1705/951.2307/951.1297
                            Telegram: Libreste Caracas

Subscription to OECD periodicals may also be
placed through main subscription agencies.

Les abonnements aux publications périodiques de
l'OCDE peuvent être souscrits auprès des
principales agences d'abonnement.

Orders and inquiries from countries where Distribu-
tors have not yet been appointed should be sent to:
OECD Publications Service, 2 rue André-Pascal,
75775 Paris Cedex 16, France.

Les commandes provenant de pays où l'OCDE n'a
pas encore désigné de distributeur peuvent être
adressées à : OCDE, Service des Publications,
2, rue André-Pascal, 75775 Paris Cedex 16, France.

7-1995

OECD PUBLICATIONS, 2 rue André-Pascal, 75775 PARIS CEDEX 16
PRINTED IN FRANCE
(21 95 10 1) ISBN 92-64-14565-6 - No. 48187 1995